CAMBRIDGE STUDIES IN LINGUISTICS
SUPPLEMENTARY VOLUME

Form and meaning in word formation

A study of Afrikaans reduplication

In this series

15 RUTH M. KEMPSON: *Presupposition and the delimitation of semantics**
16 JAMES R. HURFORD: *The linguistic theory of numerals*
17 ROGER LASS: *English phonology and phonological theory*
18 G. M. AWBERY: *The syntax of Welsh*
19 R. M. W. DIXON: *A grammar of Yidiɲ*
20 JAMES FOLEY: *Foundations of theoretical phonology*
21 A. RADFORD: *Italian syntax: transformational and relational grammar*
22 DIETER WUNDERLICH: *Foundations of linguistics**
23 DAVID W. LIGHTFOOT: *Principles of diachronic syntax**
24 ANNETTE KARMILOFF-SMITH: *A functional approach to child language**
25 PER LINELL: *Psychological reality in phonology*
26 CHRISTINE TANZ: *Studies in the acquisition of deictic terms*
28 TORBEN THRANE: *Referential-semantic analysis*
29 TAMSIN DONALDSON: *Ngiyambaa*
30 KRISTJÁN ÁRNASON: *Quality in historical phonology*
31 JOHN LAVER: *The phonetic description of voice quality*
32 PETER AUSTIN: *A grammar of Diyari, South Australia*
33 ALICE C. HARRIS: *Georgian syntax*
34 SUZANNE ROMAINE: *Socio-historical linguistics*
35 MARTIN ATKINSON: *Explanations in the study of child language development**
36 SUZANNE FLEISCHMAN: *The future in thought and language*
37 JENNY CHESHIRE: *Variation in an English dialect*
38 WILLIAM A. FOLEY and ROBERT D. VAN VALIN JR: *Functional syntax and universal grammar**
39 MICHAEL A. COVINGTON: *Syntactic theory in the High Middle Ages*
40 KENNETH J. SAFIR: *Syntactic chains*
41 J. MILLER: *Semantics and syntax*
42 H. C. BUNT: *Mass terms and model-theoretic semantics*
43 HEINZ J. GIEGERICH: *Metrical phonology and phonological structure*
44 JOHN HAIMAN: *Natural syntax*
45 BARBARA M. HORVATH: *Variation in Australian English: the sociolects of Sydney*
46 GRANT GOODALL: *Parallel structures in syntax: coordination, causatives, and restructuring*
47 JOHN M. ANDERSON and COLIN J. EWEN: *Principles of dependency phonology*
48 BARBARA A. FOX: *Discourse structure and anaphora*
49 LAUREL J. BRINTON: *The development of English aspectual systems*

Supplementary Volumes

BRIAN D. JOSEPH: *The synchrony and diachrony of the Balkan infinitive*
ANNETTE SCHMIDT: *Young people's Dyirbal: an example of language death from Australia*
JOHN HARRIS: *Phonological variation and change: studies in Hiberno-English*
TERENCE MCKAY: *Infinitival complements in German*
STELLA MARIS BORTONI-RICARDO: *The urbanization of rural dialect speakers: a socio-linguistic study in Brazil*
RUDOLF P. BOTHA: *Form and meaning in word formation: a study of Afrikaans reduplication*

Earlier titles not listed are also available
** Issued in hard covers and as paperback*

FORM AND MEANING IN WORD FORMATION

A study of Afrikaans reduplication

RUDOLF P. BOTHA
Professor of General Linguistics
University of Stellenbosch

The right of the
University of Cambridge
to print and sell
all manner of books
was granted by
Henry VIII in 1534.
The University has printed
and published continuously
since 1584.

CAMBRIDGE UNIVERSITY PRESS
CAMBRIDGE
NEW YORK NEW ROCHELLE
MELBOURNE SYDNEY

CAMBRIDGE UNIVERSITY PRESS
Cambridge, New York, Melbourne, Madrid, Cape Town, Singapore, São Paulo

Cambridge University Press
The Edinburgh Building, Cambridge CB2 2RU, UK

Published in the United States of America by Cambridge University Press, New York

www.cambridge.org
Information on this title: www.cambridge.org/9780521352604

First published 1988
This digitally printed first paperback version 2006

A catalogue record for this publication is available from the British Library

Library of Congress Cataloguing in Publication data

Botha, Rudolf P.
Form and meaning in word formation.
"Cambridge studies in linguistics. Supplementary
volume" – Ser. t.p.
Bibliography: p.
Includes index.
1. Afrikaans language – Reduplication. 2. Afrikaans
language – Word formation. I. Botha Rudolf P.
Galilean analysis of Afrikaans reduplication.
II. Cambridge studies in linguistics. III. Title.
PF861.B674 1988 439.3′65 87-26811

ISBN-13 978-0-521-35260-4 hardback
ISBN-10 0-521-35260-6 hardback

ISBN-13 978-0-521-02613-0 paperback
ISBN-10 0-521-02613-X paperback

To Henk Schultink

Contents

Acknowledgments

Various people and institutions generously assisted me in undertaking and completing this study.

A first version - informally distributed as A Galilean Analysis of Afrikaans Reduplication (= Stellenbosch Papers in Linguistics 13, 1984) - benefited considerably from questions, comments and suggestions by Henk Schultink, Peter Mühlhäusler, Paul Roberge, Walter Winckler, Cecile le Roux, Thereza Botha, and Avril Gardiner. The present revised and extended version owes its existence to constructive criticisms of the first version by Professors Mark Aronoff, Ray Jackendoff, John Lyons, Suzanne Romaine, Wolfgang Dressler and, again, Peter Mühlhäusler. Quite a number of the questions they raised were simply too hard to deal with satisfactorily. I have no adequate means for expressing my thanks to both the former and the latter friends and colleagues for the way in which they gave me access to their knowledge and considerable capacities. Had I been able to exploit these to the full, the limitations of the present version of this study would have been less severe.

As far as material support is concerned, I owe a debt of gratitude to the University of Stellenbosch for study leave and various research grants, the Alexander von Humboldt-Stiftung for a Europe Fellowship, Wolfson College (Oxford) for a Temporary Fellowship, the Technische Universität Berlin for various forms of assistance, and the Human Sciences Research Council of South Africa for a senior grant. Without the assistance of these institutions, this study could never have been completed. I hasten to add that they cannot be held responsible in any way for the opinions and conclusions presented in it.

Finally, there is my secretary and family. To Mrs. L. Gildenhuys I would like to express my thanks for the most able way in which she typed and retyped the various versions of the manuscript. And Hanna, Elizabeth and Philip deserve much more than a brief mention for allowing me once again to do my own rather peculiar thing.

Stellenbosch R.P.B.
July 1986

1 Introduction

This study is ultimately concerned with the way in which morphological form, semantic interpretation, and conceptual structure interlink in the domain of word formation. It pursues this concern by analyzing Afrikaans reduplication in the Galilean style. To proceed in this way requires the ultimate concern to be broken down into three concerns of a more immediate and specific sort: a grammatical, a general linguistic, and a metascientific one.

The grammatical or language-specific concern of this study is with the form and meaning of Afrikaans reduplications. Reduplication in Afrikaans has conventionally been taken to be a process that forms expressions such as those underscored in (1)(a)-(k).

(1) (a) Die kinders drink bottels-bottels limonade.
the children drink bottles bottles lemonade
"The children drink bottles and bottles of lemonade."

(b) Hulle speel weer bal - bal.
they play again ball ball
"They are playing their ball game again."

(c) Die pad was ent - ent sleg.
the road was stretch stretch bad
"The road was bad in some (scattered) stretches."

(d) Sy kruk - kruk stadig oor die woelige straat.
she crutch crutch slowly across the busy street
"She moves slowly on her crutches across the busy street."

(e) Die dokter vat - vat aan die swelsel.
the doctor touch touch on the swelling
"The doctor tentatively feels the swelling a couple of times."

(f) Die leeu loop brul-brul weg.
the lion walk roar roar away
"Roaring repeatedly, the lion walks away."

(g) Hulle eet dik - dik snye brood.
they eat thick thick slices bread
"They eat thumping thick slices of bread."

(h) Sy het amper - amper haar been gebreek.
she has nearly nearly her leg broken
"She very nearly broke her leg."

(i) Die ongeluk het hier-hier gebeur.
the accident has here here happened
"The accident happened right here."

(j) Hy dra tien-tien boeke die trap op.
he carry ten ten books the stairs up
"He carries the books up the stairs ten at a time."

(k) Die bulle storm drie - drie deur die hek.
the bulls charge three three through the gate
"The bulls are charging through the gate three at a time."

As a productive means of word formation, Afrikaans reduplication is a process of extraordinary complexity, from both the synchronic and the genetic points of view. This is the conclusion that seems to emerge from conventional analyses such as those by Scholtz (1963), Botha (1964), Kempen (1969), and Raidt (1981). From the synchronic point of view the process, on these analyses, applies to forms representing a variety of lexical categories. These include nouns (as in (1)(a), (b), (c), and (d)), verbs (as in (1)(e), and (f)), adjectives (as in (1)(g)), adverbs (as in (1)(h) and (i)), and numerals (as in (1)(j) and (k)). The process, moreover, creates diverse types of exocentric forms: adverbs based on nouns (as in (1)(c)), verbs based on nouns (as in (1)(d)), adverbs based on verbs (as in (1)(f)), and adverbs based on numerals (as in (1)(k)), to mention only a few. And on such conventional analyses the meanings said to be expressed by reduplication in Afrikaans are stunningly diverse. These include, amongst others, "considerable number" (as in (1)(a)), "limited number" and "distribution" (as in (1)(c)), "iteration" (as in (1)(e) and (f)), "simultaneity" (as in (1)(f)), "intensity" (as in (1)(g) and (h)), "collectivity" and "serial ordering" (as in (1)(j) and (k)), and "emphasis" (as in (1)(i)). In some cases (as in (1)(b)) reduplication has been claimed not to express any cognitive or referential "meaning" at all. In sum, then, conventional analyses characterize Afrikaans reduplication as an uncommonly complex process, both formally and semantically. In order to "account" for the presumed formal and semantic complexities of Afrikaans reduplication, the conventional analyses, being nongenerative, have set up elaborate taxonomies.

Within a broader perspective, however, the conclusion that Afrikaans reduplication is such a highly complex phenomenon synchronically does not necessarily ring true. There are different kinds of evidence that, as a property of language in general, reduplication constitutes one of the simpler, more natural means of word formation. Thus, reduplication is generally used as a means of word formation in certain reduced types of language (known also as "simplified registers") such as baby-talk, foreigner talk, broken language and pidgins.[1] In addition reduplication is a means of word formation that manifests a measure of iconicity: form and meaning resemble each other in a quantitative respect, which is to say that the form of reduplications is in a sense non-arbitrary or motivated. So the complexity of reduplication in Afrikaans appears to be in conflict with the relative simplicity of reduplication as a means of word formation in language in general.

As regards its grammatical concern, then, the present study will argue that the synchronic complexity of Afrikaans reduplication is in fact in the eye of the beholder. Specifically, this study will present a lexicalist analysis of Afrikaans reduplication in the Galilean style postulating only one unifying formation rule and only one unifying interpretation rule, both of which are quite simple and general. As regards the formation rule, it will be shown that much of the apparent formal complexity of Afrikaans reduplication disappears if this rule is (a) made subject to certain general conditions on word formation rules, and (b) applied in conjunction with other rules of Afrikaans grammar. Not only these general conditions but also these other rules have to be postulated independently of an analysis of Afrikaans reduplication. In motivating the rule of formation, I will show how the willingness of conventional analyses to assign unmotivated claims the status of grammatical facts has contributed to the apparent formal complexity of Afrikaans reduplication. A parallel argument will be presented for the interpretation rule. Specifically, it will be shown that the semantics of Afrikaans reduplication becomes quite transparent if this rule is allowed to interact (a) with other aspects of the semantic structure of Afrikaans, and (b) with general principles of conceptual structure, formulated as conceptualization rules.

This brings us to the general-linguistic concern of this study: to gain, through the Galilean analysis of Afrikaans reduplication, a better understanding (a) of language-independent formal principles of word formation, and (b) of the way in which general principles of semantic and conceptual structure interact in determining the meanings of morphologically complex words. In its concern with the former principles of word formation, the analysis of reduplication presented in this study is related to such analyses of reduplication as those by Carrier (1979), McCarthy (1979, 1981), Lieber (1981), Marantz (1982) and Thomas-Flinders (1983). The postulated general principles of semantic and conceptual structure on which the present analysis of the semantics of Afrikaans reduplications hinges will be shown to be compatible with Jackendoff's (1983) new theory of meaning and conceptual structure. These principles of conceptual structure are formulated as conceptualization rules, a distinct kind of device pertinent to the interpretation of linguistic expressions.

In pursuing both its language-specific and its language-independent concerns, the study will attempt "to make the minimal special assumptions or statements about reduplication", to take over a recent formulation of Marantz's (1982:436). The use of exotic theoretical devices will be consistently avoided: the need for such devices will be taken as symptomatic of insufficient understanding of the phenomenon under consideration.

It was mentioned above that Afrikaans reduplication has been considered an extraordinarily complex phenomenon from a genetic point of view too. The fact that Afrikaans makes extensive use of lexically diverse types of reduplication has been considered a major problem in conventional studies such as those noted above. These studies have assumed that Afrikaans is a language that developed from Dutch dialects spoken at the Cape in the seventeenth century. Yet, in the case of various types of Afrikaans reduplication - for example, those illustrated in (1)(c), (f) and (k) - there is no evidence at all of their use by the dialect speakers who were at the Cape at the time when Afrikaans was coming into being. In addition, reduplications of these types are unacceptable in Modern Standard Dutch and have, on those grounds, been labeled "un-Dutch" in some of these studies. It has been claimed in fact that there is no Indo-Germanic language that even approaches Afrikaans in its use of reduplication as a productive means of word formation.[2]

Certain scholars have assigned the "un-Dutch" types of Afrikaans reduplication the status of products of creolization - reflecting the influence of Creole Portuguese, Malay dialects or some other (substratum) language(s) on the seventeenth-century Dutch dialects spoken at the Cape.[3] It has been claimed, for example, that Malay has types of reduplication that are similar to, and that gave rise to, the "un-Dutch" types found in Afrikaans. This "creole" account of the origin of the latter forms has been treated with considerable reservation in the most influential of the conventional studies, however. Kempen (1969), for example, is highly skeptical about it. And Scholtz (1963), though not rejecting all versions of this account out of hand, finds it necessary to invoke a notion of "spontaneous origin" to "explain" the genesis of the "un-Dutch" types of Afrikaans reduplication. Thus, for certain types of Afrikaans reduplication, conventional studies have not been able either to establish a "Dutch" origin or to accept a "creole" origin.[4] From a genetic point of view, then, Afrikaans reduplication also appears to be a phenomenon of considerable complexity.

The question of the genesis of Afrikaans reduplication, unfortunately, cannot be a concern of the present study. It may be noted, though, that the synchronic analysis presented in this study has obvious implications for the study of the genesis of this word-formation process. Specifically, this study reveals that conventional studies of the origin of Afrikaans reduplication proceeded from descriptively inadequate synchronic analyses of the phenomenon. That is to say, these studies attempted to unravel the origin and developmental history of a phenomenon whose nature and properties they seriously misunderstood. These studies, moreover, were not carried out within the framework of an adequate general theory of language contact. It is therefore not unreasonable to expect that, on further investigation, the diachronic complexity of Afrikaans reduplication too will turn out to be illusory. This complexity may be no more than a by-product of attempts to trace the origin and development of a phenomenon that belongs to the realm of the unreal.

Thereby we have come to the metascientific concern of this study: to provide a concrete illustration of the heuristic potential of the Galilean style of inquiry. In Botha (1982:42) I argued that the expression "the Galilean style" may be used, with certain reservations, to denote a mode of linguistic inquiry that entails the following:

(2) (a) To make progress in the scientific study of language (and mind), we should set, as the fundamental aim of inquiry, depth of understanding in restricted areas - and not gross coverage of data.

(b) To get serious inquiry started, we should make radical abstractions and idealizations in defining the initial scope of the inquiry.

(c) To capture the desired understanding or insight, we need unifying, principled theories deductively removed (perhaps far removed) from the problematic data.

(d) To keep up the momentum of the inquiry, we should adopt an attitude of epistemological tolerance towards promising theories that are threatened by still unexplained or apparently negative data.

I claimed, moreover, that this style of inquiry, as practiced by leading generative syntacticians, could not yet be extended to morphological and semantic analysis. This claim was based on the observation that morphology and semantics at the time lacked the kinds of generalizations that could lead to the formulation of genuine unifying principles. The work that I have since done on Afrikaans reduplication, however, has led me to believe that it is possible to achieve a significant measure of theoretical unification in morphological and semantic analysis too.

As regards (2)(c), I will show how the use of the Galilean style makes it possible to increase our insight into the form and meaning of Afrikaans reduplications through the formulation of unifying theories of formation and interpretation, respectively. And in regard to (2)(d), I will show how an unwillingness to reject such theories out of hand in the light of "recalcitrant" linguistic data could lead to the discovery that these data had no factual basis whatsoever and, consequently, never posed a real threat to the theories. The Galilean style will be shown, in other words, to be a powerful tool for weeding out fictions dressed up as facts. At the same time, therefore, the view that depth of insight is necessarily pursued at the cost of factual accuracy will be shown up as a myth. The reverse view, as a matter of fact, will suggest itself: pursuing depth of insight leads to an increase in factual accuracy. In sum: the metascientific concern of this study is to show that the Galilean style may be fruitfully applied in every area where depth of insight is sought. Less well researched areas, such as morphology and semantics, also lend themselves to the profitable use of this style of inquiry; its considerable heuristic power is by no means realizable in the more advanced areas, such as syntax, only.[5]

This brings us to the organization of the present study. In addition to this, introductory, chapter it contains four more chapters. Whereas Chapter 2 presents a (synchronic) analysis of the formation of Afrikaans reduplications, Chapter 3 develops an analysis of the semantics of these forms. Chapter 4 deals with the manner in which these analyses tie in with each other. The concluding chapter, Chapter 5, retrospectively considers the ways in which both analyses instantiate the Galilean style of linguistic inquiry. Readers who wish to gain a better general idea of the scope and substance of this study before plunging into the specifics of the following chapters may begin by taking a look at the retrospective paragraphs 2.10 and 3.16, and Chapter 5.

Before turning to the theories of the formation and interpretation of Afrikaans reduplications, it is necessary to say something about the origin of the Afrikaans data that will be presented in subsequent sections of this study. I have found conventional studies such as those by Scholtz (1963), Kempen (1969), and Raidt (1981) to be rich sources of intuitive observations about both the well-formedness and the interpretation of Afrikaans reduplications. Though I do not accept the analyses presented in these studies of Afrikaans reduplication, I have used many of their intuitive observations for the purpose of illustrating problems and checking the adequacy of my solutions for these problems. By drawing on these observations, I have sought to provide a firmer and more independent empirical basis for my theories of formation and interpretation. In cases where I found observations of conventional studies to be unclear in import or in conflict with my own judgments or hypotheses, I carefully consulted the linguistic intuitions of both ordinary and linguistically trained native speakers. In accordance with standard practice, I did not use specially devised behavioral or operational tests for this purpose. As argued elsewhere (e.g., Botha 1973:§5.4.3), little is to be gained by checking the accuracy of linguistic intuitions with the aid of tests whose validity and reliability are obscure for principled reasons. This study, in fact, furnishes support for the general view that one of the more reliable indications of the accuracy or relevance of a given linguistic intuition is found in its fit with a principled and unifying theory. Conflict between a linguistic intuition and a prediction by such a theory often indicates that the intuition is either incorrect or irrelevant to the appraisal of the theory.

2 Formation

2.1 Outline

To account for the formal properties of Afrikaans reduplications the theory to be developed below has to express the following generalization:

(1) Afrikaans reduplications are words formed by the copying of words.

This generalization may be expressed by means of two hypotheses: the rule stated informally in (2)(a) - or less informally in (2)(b) - and the status specification in (3).

(2) (a) Copy α

(b) $\alpha_i \rightarrow [\alpha_i \; \alpha_i]$

(3) (2) is a word formation rule

It will be argued below that, if the formation rule (2) is applied in conjunction with other, independently motivated rules of Afrikaans grammar and if, moreover, it is made subject to certain independently motivated general linguistic conditions, only a minimum of additional language-specific assumptions are needed to account for the formal properties of Afrikaans reduplications. Moreover, if word formation rules (or WFRs) are formally distinct from other formation rules, then (3) need not be stipulated as a separate claim in the grammar of Afrikaans.

The justification for the theory of the formation of Afrikaans reduplications to be presented in subsequent paragraphs has two basic components, each complementary to the other. On the one hand this theory has a highly desirable conceptual property: it provides insight into what appears to be a bewilderingly complex phenomenon by reducing its apparent complexity to a minimal number of hypotheses that are both simple and general. In achieving this reduction, the theory gains considerably in unifying power. On the other hand the theory has highly desirable empirical credentials: it implies correct consequences. That is, the hypotheses (2) and (3), in conjunction with other, independently required language-specific and language-independent assumptions, make correct predictions about the properties of a natural class of Afrikaans morphologically complex words.

2.2 Category type of reduplications

Let us begin by considering the theory's predictions about the category type of reduplications as a whole, i.e., the category type of $[\alpha_i \ \alpha_i]$. Hypothesis (3) states that the rule (2) is a word formation rule. The theory therefore predicts that

(4) Afrikaans reduplications have the status of (morphologically complex) words.[1]

This prediction may be tested under the standard assumption that morphologically complex words are characterized by a property that may be called "internal integrity": certain grammatical processes may apply to words as wholes but not to the constituents of words. This generally held assumption may be formulated somewhat more precisely as "The Morphological Island Constraint".

(5) The individual constituents of morphologically complex words are not accessible to inflectional, derivational or syntactic processes.[2]

This condition accounts for the fact that reordering the constituents of morphologically complex words or interrupting them by the insertion of other elements results in strings that are ill-formed.

Considered against this background, the prediction (4) is borne out by the fact that individual constituents of Afrikaans reduplications cannot be inflected or syntactically modified and, as a result, separated from each other by intervening elements. Thus, whereas the reduplication ent-ent as a whole can be inflected with the plural suffix -e, its individual constituents - e.g. the first one - cannot be so inflected:[3]

(6) (a) Die pad was ent - ent sleg.
the road was stretch stretch bad
(b) Die pad was [ent - ent] + E sleg.
the road was [stretch stretch] + es bad
(c) Die pad was *[ent + E] - ent sleg.
the road was [stretch + es] stretch bad

Again, the reduplication vat-vat as a whole can be inflected with the past tense prefix ge-, but its individual constituents - e.g. the second one - cannot be so inflected.

(7) (a) Die dokter vat - vat aan die swelsel.
the doctor touch touch on the swelling
(b) Die dokter het aan die swelsel GE + [vat - vat].
the doctor has on the swelling AFFIX + [touch touch]
(c) Die dokter het aan die swelsel *vat - [GE + vat].
the doctor has on the swelling touch [AFFIX + touch]

In (6)(c) and (7)(c) the affixes separate the constituents of the reduplications and cause the resulting strings to be ill-formed. This ill-formedness can be explained on the assumption that reduplications are complex words whose internal integrity may not be violated. The ill-formedness of the strings in (6)(c) and (7)(c) therefore bears out the prediction (4).

Notice, incidentally, that the distinction between inflection and derivation used above is the one used conventionally in the discussion of Afrikaans morphology. On this distinction the affixes indicating number (in the case of nouns), tense (in the case of verbs), and comparison (in the case of adjectives and adverbs) represent inflectional affixes. The question of how to draw the distinction between inflection and derivation within an explanatory theory of morphology, of course, is a quite complex one that has given rise to a considerable amount of controversy in generative morphology, as is evidenced by studies such as those by, for example, Halle (1973), Siegel (1974), Aronoff (1976), Lieber (1981), Selkirk

(1982), Anderson (1982), and Thomas-Flinders (1983). The present study will steer clear of this controversy since nothing of significance hinges on whether number, tense or comparison represent inflectional or derivational categories in Afrikaans. All that matters here is whether a number, tense or comparison affix may or may not interrupt a string that appears to be a morphologically complex word. If such interruption were possible the string in question would lack a fundamental property of (morphologically complex) words, viz. internal integrity. This study will therefore use "inflection" and related terms in the conventional sense as pretheoretical descriptive devices.

The prediction that Afrikaans reduplications have the status of (morphologically complex) words is borne out also by the fact that individual constituents of these reduplications cannot be modified syntactically. For example, whereas the reduplication amper-amper as a whole can be modified by so, its second constituent cannot take this modifier.

(8) (a) Sy het amper - amper haar been gebreek.
she has nearly nearly her leg broken
(b) Sy het so amper - amper haar been gebreek.
she has so nearly nearly her leg broken
(c) Sy het *amper - [so amper] haar been gebreek.
she has nearly [so nearly] her leg broken

To assess the acceptability of a string such as (8)(c), the reduplication with the internal modifier must be spoken with the tempo and the stress pattern that typically distinguish reduplications from lexically related syntactic repetitions. That is, the reduplication must be spoken at a fast tempo without any marked pause between the constituents, and the constituents must be evenly stressed.[4] Spoken with heavy emphasis on both the first and the second amper and with a marked pause between the first amper and so, (8)(c) is acceptable. The constituent with these properties is not a word, however, but a syntactic phrase. In the syntactic phrase amper, so amper (meaning "nearly, so nearly"), the repetition of amper has the function of emphasizing the semantic content of amper. In the word amper-amper the reduplication of amper has the function of intensifying the expression of the notion "nearly".

The prediction that Afrikaans reduplications are (morphologically complex) words can be checked against a second set of data. In Afrikaans both morphologically simple and morphologically complex words may constitute bases for (further) word formation. Taken in conjunction with this generalization, the prediction (4) implies the further claim that Afrikaans reduplications can constitute bases for other word formation processes. And this claim is correct, as is indicated by (9)(b), (10)(b), and (11)(b), in which the underscored derived words are based on the reduplications in (9)(a), (10)(a), and (11)(a) respectively.

(9) (a) Die dokter vat - vat aan die swelsel.
the doctor touch touch on the swelling

(b) Die dokter se GE + [vat - vat] aan die swelsel ontstel hom.
the doctor's AFFIX + [touch touch] on the swelling upset him
"The way the doctor repeatedly/tentatively touches the swelling upsets him."

(10) (a) Hy steier dronk-dronk die kamer binne.
he stagger drunk drunk the room into
"He staggers drunkenly into the room."

(b) Hy steier [dronk-dronk] + ERIG die kamer binne.
he stagger [drunk drunk] + AFFIX the room into
"He staggers slightly drunkenly into the room."

(11) (a) Die hond knor - knor vir die besoeker.
the dog growl growl for the visitor
"The dog growls repeatedly at the visitor."

(b) Die [knor - knor] + DERY van die hond maak hom bang.
the [growl growl] + AFFIX of the dog make him afraid
"He is frightened by the way the dog keeps growling."

Afrikaans reduplications can be used as constituents of compounds too, as is indicated by the forms underscored in (12)-(14).

(12) (a) Hulle speel weer bal - bal.
they play again ball ball
(b) Hulle verander die [bal - bal] + reëls elke dag.
they change the [ball ball] + rules every day
"They change the rules of the ball game every day."

(13) (a) Sy het amper - amper haar been gebreek.
she has nearly nearly her leg broken
(b) Gelukig sterf mense nie in [amper - amper] + ongelukke nie.
fortunately die people not in [nearly nearly] + accidents not
"Fortunately, people are not killed in near accidents."

(14) (a) Hy dra tien - tien boeke die trap op.
he carries ten ten books the stairs up
"He carries the books up the stairs ten at a time."
(b) Moenie van die [tien-tien] + patroon afwyk nie.
must not from the [ten ten] + pattern deviate not
"Don't deviate from the ten-at-a-time pattern."

Note that the fact that Afrikaans reduplications may constitute bases of derived words and compounds shows up an aspect of the interrelatedness of the formation rule (2) on the one hand and Afrikaans affixation and compounding rules on the other hand:

(15) (Assuming that all these rules are in the same component of the grammar,) the formation rule (2) must be capable of feeding the affixation and compounding rules.

The question arises, of course, whether the formation rule (2), in turn, is fed by the other types of morphological rules, and, moreover, whether the formation rule feeds itself too. To these questions we will turn in §§2.3 and 2.8 below.

2.3 Category type of bases

We come now to the category type of the forms on which reduplications are based, i.e. the category type of α. Recall once more that hypothesis (3) states that the rule of Afrikaans reduplication is a word formation rule. Following Aronoff (1976:21), lexicalist morphologists have assumed a general constraint on WFRs that may be called "The Word-base Constraint".[5]

(16) All regular word formation processes are word-based.

This formulation of the constraint entails that a new word is formed by applying a regular WFR to a single word.[6] Both units smaller than words, e.g., stems and roots, and units larger than words, e.g., syntactic phrases, are precluded by (16) as possible bases for word formation.[7] In conjunction with (16), the hypothesis (3) has the following consequence.

(17) The bases to which the rule of Afrikaans reduplication applies must be words.

This prediction is borne out by the facts.

Segments of words cannot be reduplicated in Afrikaans. This is why Kempen (1969), in compiling his large corpus of reduplications used in literary Afrikaans, found a mere handful of "reduplications" in which one of the constituents represents only a part of the other.

(18) glim - [glim + lag]
gleam gleam laugh
"smile faintly"
struik - struikelend
(meaningless stumbling
segment)
"stumbling badly"
[die + selfde] - selfde
the same same
"the very same"

Kempen (1969:180) is at pains to point out that forms such as (18) are unique, representing literary devices used by an author whose "language" is not "perfect Afrikaans". Parts of words - e.g., syllables, non-syllabic sound sequences, morphemic constituents, etc. - cannot be reduplicated in spoken Afrikaans either.[8]

In testing the prediction that Afrikaans reduplications are word-based, a particular distinction has to be kept in mind, namely the distinction between reduplication and onomatopoeic repetition. According to Marchand (1969:81), the latter phenomenon involves the "repetition of non-independent expressive signs" and is illustrated by the English clap-clap (of hoofs), click-click (of a needle), chuff-chuff (of an engine), etc. Viewed against the background of the distinction between reduplication and onomatopoeic repetition, forms such as those underscored in (19) are not counter-examples to the claim that Afrikaans reduplications are word-based.

(19) (a) 'n Tinktinkie sit op die heining.
a grass-warbler sit on the fence
"A grass-warbler sits on the fence."

(b) Die hoep-hoep maak in die hol boomstam nes.
the hoopoe makes in the hollow tree trunk nest
"The hoopoe is building its nest in the hollow tree trunk."

(c) Die djap-djappie maak in die vyeboom nes.
the thrush make in the fig tree nest
"The thrush builds its nest in the fig tree."

The repeated constituents - tink, hoep and djap - of the underscored forms in (19) are not used as independent words in Afrikaans. But then, as is clear from Kempen's (1969:248ff.) discussion of forms such as the underscored ones, their primary function is onomatopoeic and they do not have the properties typical of reduplications. An onomatopoeic form may of course be a possible independent word and thus constitute a base for reduplication. We will return to this point in §2.5 below.

Note that the prediction (17) does not restrict the bases of Afrikaans reduplication to morphologically simple words. On the contrary, it expresses the claim that morphologically complex words can be reduplicated too. The essence of this claim is correct: inflected words, derived words, and compounds may form bases of the formation rule (2). To begin with inflected words, we may now glance back at (1)(a) in Chapter 1 to observe that the base of bottels-bottels is the inflected word bottel + s (= "bottle" + PLURAL); the underscored nominal reduplications in (20)(a)-(c) are likewise based on words inflected for plural.

(20) (a) Uit die lug sien jy [heuwel + S]-[heuwel + S]
from the air see you hill + PLUR hill + PLUR
net waar jy kyk.
just where you look
"From the air one sees hill upon hill wherever one looks."

(b) Hy het [hap + E] - [hap + E] afgesluk.
he has bite + PLUR bite + PLUR down swallowed
"He gulped the stuff down by the mouthful."

(c) Die pad was [ent + E] - [ent + E] sleg.
the road was stretch + PLUR stretch + PLUR bad
"The road was bad in quite a few stretches."

Turning to another lexical class, we next observe that Afrikaans has adjectival reduplications that are based on superlatives also formed by means of inflection.

(21) (a) Net die [ryk + STE] - [ryk + STE] mense kan gaan.
only the rich + SUPERL rich + SUPERL people can go
"Only the very richest people can go."

(b) Hy kweek die [mooi + STE] - [mooi + STE]
he grows the lovely + SUPERL lovely + SUPERL
proteas.
proteas
"He grows ever such lovely proteas."

Suppose that, within the framework of a principled general distinction between inflection and derivation, the affixes expressing number and comparison (comparative -er and superlative -ste) had to be denied the status of inflectional affixes in Afrikaans. Such a finding would not refute the claim that Afrikaans reduplications may be based on inflected forms. It would merely narrow down the scope of the claim by restricting the number of inflectional affixes in Afrikaans. To refute this claim one would have to be able to show that there are Afrikaans reduplications which are ill-formed in virtue of the fact that they are based on inflected forms. But notice that to say that Afrikaans reduplications can be based on inflected forms is, of course, not to say that all reduplications based on inflected forms are acceptable. To this point I return in Chapter 4 below.

Derived words and compounds may also serve as bases for the rule (2) of Afrikaans reduplication. The reduplications in (22) have derived words as bases; those in (23) are based on compounds.

(22) (a) Hulle speel [voet+JIE]-[voet+JIE].
they play foot+DIM foot+DIM
(where DIM = diminutive suffix)
"They play a courting game with their feet."

(b) Hy [HER + kou]-[HER + kou] nog aan die antwoord.
he RE + chew RE + chew still on the reply
"He is still ruminating over the reply."

(c) [Moed + ELOOS]-[moed + ELOOS] skud hy sy kop.
courage+LESS courage+LESS shake he his head
"He shakes his head in utter discouragement."

(23) (a) [Skeeps+vragte]-[skeeps+vragte] masjinerie lê op die kaai.
ship +loads ship +loads machinery lie on the quay
"Any number of shiploads of machinery are lying on the quay."

(b) Hy loop [stywe+been]-[stywe+been] die straat af.
he walks stiff+leg stiff+leg the street down
"He goes down the street, his leg(s) as stiff as anything."

(c) [Net +nou]-[net +nou] val jy van die stoel af.
just+now just+now fall you of the chair off
"Careful, or the next thing you know you'll be falling off the chair."

(d) Die kinders speel [tand +arts]-[tand +arts].
the children play tooth doctor tooth doctor
"The children are playing 'at the dentist's'."

The discussion above, in fact, sheds light on a second aspect of the way in which Afrikaans reduplication is interrelated with other word formation rules of the language:[9]

(24) The rules of inflection, derivation, and compounding must be able to feed the formation rule (2).

Note that (24), like (15), does not specify that the formation rule (2) can or cannot feed itself. This appears to be an ad hoc omission, a point that will be taken up again in §2.8 below.

We still have to consider the second part of the prediction (17), i.e. the part that excludes units larger than words from the category of possible bases of the Afrikaans reduplication rule (2). This part, too, is borne out by the relevant data. Though syntactic phrases may, for emphasis, be repeated to form more complex syntactic units, they cannot be reduplicated in Afrikaans to form morphologically complex words. Thus, whereas the underscored strings in (25)(b) and (26)(b) are well-formed as syntactic phrases, they are unacceptable as reduplications.

(25) (a) Hulle eet baie dik snye brood.
they eat very thick slices bread
"They eat very thick slices of bread."

(b) Hulle eet [baie dik] - [baie dik] snye brood.
they eat [very thick] [very thick] slices bread

(26) (a) Ons beleef moeilike tye.
we experience difficult times
"We are experiencing difficult times."

(b) Ons beleef [moeilike tye] - [moeilike tye].
we experience [difficult times] [difficult times]

Pronounced with a heavy stress on the appropriate constituents and a distinct pause between them, the underscored forms of (25)(b) and (26)(b) can be used to emphasize or dramatize the content of the corresponding unrepeated phrases of (25)(a) and

(26)(a). The underscored forms in (25)(b) and (26)(b), however, cannot be pronounced at a fast rate with non-emphatic stress - i.e., with the phonetic form of reduplications - to express intensity or increased quantity.

One last point: there is no need for the formation rule (2) to stipulate that it takes words as bases only. This stipulation is provided for by the language-independent Word-base Constraint (16).

2.4 Category type of constituents

With respect to category type, Afrikaans reduplications may be characterized as words formed by the reduplication of words. But what is the category type of the constituents of these reduplications? Must the category status of Word be assigned to the constituents too? What, for example, is the category status of the left-hand constituent ent (= "stretch") and the right-hand constituent ent of the reduplication ent-ent in (1)(c) of Chapter 1, or that of the left-hand constituent vat (= "touch") and the right-hand constituent vat of the reduplication vat-vat in (1)(e) of Chapter 1?

In the case of these questions, too, the answer can be derived from the formation theory of Afrikaans reduplication. Recall that the status assigned on this theory to reduplications as wholes is that of morphologically complex words. And in conjunction with the independently motivated Morphological Island Constraint (5) this theory makes the following prediction:

(27) The constituents of Afrikaans reduplications do not have the status of words.

It is a property of Afrikaans words that they may constitute bases for (further) word formation. But the Morphological Island Constraint makes the constituents of reduplications - which are complex words on our theory - inaccessible to inflectional, derivational and syntactic processes. Hence, it is predicted that these constituents will not be words.

The prediction (27) is correct. For example, ent (= "stretch") as an independent word may be inflected for plural by the suffixation of -e, giving ent-E. And ent may also constitute a base for the diminutivization rule that affixes a form of the suffix -ie to nouns, giving ent + JIE in the case of ent. But neither of the constituents of the reduplication ent-ent can receive the plural or the diminutive suffix.

(28) (a) Die pad was *[ent + E]-ent sleg. [= (6)(c)]
(b) Die pad was *ent-[ent + E] sleg.
(c) Die pad was *[ent + JIE]-ent sleg.
(d) Die pad was *ent-[ent + JIE] sleg.

And, consonant with the prediction (27), neither constituent of the reduplication vat-vat can be a base for the rule affixing the past participle prefix ge- to verbs.

(29) (a) Die dokter het aan die swelsel *[GE-vat]-vat.
(b) Die dokter het aan die swelsel *vat-[GE-vat]. [= (7)(c)]

Again we see that, in conjunction with an independently motivated general-linguistic constraint on WFRs, the theory of the formation of Afrikaans reduplication (2)-(3) makes correct predictions about the formal properties of Afrikaans reduplications. Observe, incidentally, that the prediction (27) does not express the claim that affixes, whether inflectional or derivational, cannot occur inside reduplications. As is predicted by the theory - cf. (2), (21), (22) above - affixes may occur inside reduplications if such affixes are constituents of the input bases to which the rule of reduplication (2) applies. The reduplication gevat-gevat may therefore be formed on the basis of the inflected form gevat. Though this reduplication would be well-formed from a formal point of view, it could still be unacceptable, its unacceptability being caused by non-formal factors such as those to be considered in Chapter 4 below.

2.5 Lexical category of bases

In §2.3 it was shown why the Afrikaans formation rule (2) does not need to specify the category type of the bases (α's) to which it applies. That these bases have to be words is a consequence of the independent Word-base Constraint (16). The question now is whether the formation rule (2) needs to be elaborated so as to stipulate the lexical categories of the words ('s) to which it may apply. Fortunately, this is not necessary: these lexical categories are specified by means of a general principle, the "Open Category Constraint".

(30) The Afrikaans reduplication rule (2) applies
    (a) to words of all open lexical categories, and
    (b) to words of open lexical categories only.

The term "open (lexical) category" has been used conventionally to denote all (lexical) categories to which new members may be added and whose membership, consequently, cannot be specified exhaustively by means of a fixed list.[10]

Open lexical categories are extended primarily by the addition of morphologically complex words formed by means of general word formation processes such as compounding, affixation, conversion, etc. Secondarily, however, these categories also acquire new members in the form of borrowings, blends, clippings, acronyms, etc.[11]

In Afrikaans the open lexical categories are Noun, Verb, Adjective, Adverb and Numeral. Accordingly, the all (= (a)) clause of the Open Category Constraint, on the one hand, has the consequence that the formation rule (2) must be able to take nouns, verbs, adjectives, adverbs and numerals as bases. That this consequence is correct is indicated by (31)-(35), in which the underscored reduplications are based on nouns, verbs, adjectives, adverbs, and numerals respectively.[12]

(31) (a) Uit die lug sien jy heuwels-heuwels net waar
from the air see you hills hills just where
jy kyk. [= (20)(a)]
you look
"From the air one sees numerous hills wherever one looks."

(b) Hulle speel elke dag tol-tol.
they play every day top top
"They play (at) tops every day."

(c) Sakke-sakke meel word afgelaai.
bags bags flour are off loaded
"Bags and bags of flour are unloaded."

(32) (a) Boomer lek-lek die wond.
Boomer lick lick the wound
"Boomer tentatively licks the wound a couple of times."

(b) Die donder rammel-rammel in die verte.
the thunder rumble rumble in the distance
"A continual rumble of thunder may be heard in the distance."

(c) Hy skop-skop teen die deur.
he kick kick against the door
"He gives the door a few exploratory kicks."

(33) (a) Dit is 'n swart-swart dag in ons geskiedenis.
it is a black black day in our history
"It is one of the very blackest days in our history."

(b) Diep-diep lyne loop oor haar voorkop.
deep deep lines run across her forehead
"Deep lines cut into her brow."

(c) Die sappigste-sappigste happies is vir
the juiciest juiciest titbits are for
die gaste.
the guests
"The most mouth-watering of the titbits are for the guests."

(34) (a) Die ongeluk het hier-hier gebeur.
the accident has here here happened
"The accident happened right here."

(b) Hulle pak die taak saam - saam aan.
they set the task together together to
"They tackle the job very much as a joint effort."

(c) Die portier maak vaak - vaak die deur oop.
the porter make sleepy sleepy the door open
"The porter, slow with sleep, opens the door."

(35) (a) Hy ontvang drie - drie studente op 'n keer.
he receive three three students at a time
"He receives the students in groups of three at a time."

(b) Vyf-vyf skape bars deur die hek.
five five sheep burst through the gate
"The sheep are bursting through the gate five at a time."

(c) Die kinders is sewe - sewe huis toe gestuur.
the children were seven seven home to sent
"The children were sent home in groups of seven."

On the other hand, in terms of the only (= (b)) clause, the Open Category Constraint entails that the formation rule (2) cannot apply to words that are members of closed lexical categories. This consequence is correct too: conjunctions, determiners, prepositions, particles, etc. are not regularly reduplicated in Afrikaans. This, of course, is not to say that members of such closed categories cannot be repeated deliberately to create deviant forms for special (literary) purposes or that members of closed categories cannot be involved, as constituents of phrases, in syntactic repetition.

Kempen (1969:249) has claimed that reduplication is permissible in the case of interjections. Theories of generative syntax and morphology have not, however, assigned interjections the status of a lexical category. And even if we were to assume the existence of a lexical category of interjections, Kempen's claim that interjections may be reduplicated would not bear on the Open Category Constraint (30). This is so because the forms furnished by Kempen in support of his claim should not be analyzed as reduplicated interjections. Indeed, one subset of these forms should not be analyzed as the products of (morphological) reduplication at all, namely forms such as those in (19) - that is, tinktinkie, hoep-hoep, djapdjappie. As was argued in §2.3 above, these forms should be analyzed as products of the repetition of non-independent expressive signs, the vast majority of which are onomatopoeic.

A second subset of Kempen's forms may be analyzed as reduplications, but not as reduplications based on interjections. This point is illustrated by the underscored forms in (36).

(36) (a) Die strum - strum van die ghitaar word ver
the 'strum' 'strum' of the guitar is far
gehoor.
heard
"Thrummed with a will, the guitar could be heard far and wide."

(b) Hy gaan met 'n gerusstellende uff - uff langs
he goes with a comforting 'uff' 'uff' next to
die wyfie sit.
the female sit
"Grunting a reassurance, he sits down next to the female."

(c) Hy tweng - tweng en pang - pang aan die snare.
he 'twang' 'twang' and 'pang' 'pang' on the strings
"He was twanging and panging away on the strings."

Corresponding to the reduplications in (36)(a)-(c) are the unreduplicated forms underscored in (37)(a)-(c) respectively.

(37) (a) Die strum van die ghitaar word ver gehoor.
(b) Hy gaan met 'n gerusstellende uff langs die wyfie sit.
(c) Hy tweng en pang aan die snare.

strum in (37)(a) and uff in (37)(b) are nouns; tweng and pang in (37)(c) are verbs.[13] On the simplest analysis, one not imputing undesirable exocentricity to the Afrikaans lexicon, the reduplications strum-strum, uff-uff, tweng-tweng and pang-pang have the noun strum, the noun uff, the verb tweng and the verb pang as their respective bases. There is no obvious advantage in claiming that the bases of those reduplications are the interjections strum, uff, tweng and pang respectively. Kempen, in fact, does not provide any justification for this claim.

In sum: the forms analyzed by Kempen as reduplications based on interjections should be reanalyzed either as products of the repetition of non-independent expressive signs or as reduplications based on non-interjections. That is, his analysis does not support the claim that interjections are regularly reduplicated in Afrikaans.

We still have to consider the status of the Open Category Constraint within the framework of lexicalist morphology. To my knowledge, the notion of "open lexical category" does not play an overt role in any of the recently proposed theories of lexicalist morphology. A notion of "major lexical category", however, does. Aronoff (1976:21) has proposed a constraint on both the input to (i.e., the bases of) and the output of WFRs which may be called the "Major Category Constraint".[14]

(38) Both the new word (formed by a WFR) and the existing one (to which the WFR applies) are members of major lexical categories.

Aronoff, however, does not explicate the content of his notion of "major lexical category". Specifically, he does not indicate how this notion is related to the notions of "lexical category" and "major category" that formed part of the syntactic theories developed by Chomsky (1965, 1970) in the sixties and seventies. In _Aspects of the theory of syntax_ (1965:74), Chomsky considered N, V and M to be lexical categories. A major category he defined as "a lexical category or a category that dominates a string ... X ..., where X is a lexical category". And he took all categories except Det (and possibly M and Aux) to be major categories. Chomsky did not, however, operate with a notion of "major _lexical_ category". So, Aronoff's notion of "major lexical category" cannot be identical to either of Chomsky's _Aspects_ notions "lexical category" and "major category".

In developing the $\overline{X}$-theory, Chomsky proposed in "Remarks on nominalization" (1970:35, 52) a different set of lexical categories: N, V and A.[15] Adding P to this set, Jackendoff (1977:31) has subsequently referred to its four members as "major lexical categories". To the set of "minor lexical categories" Jackendoff (1977:32-33) had earlier assigned Adv, Prt, M, Art, Q and Deg (this last being a special class of adverbs that included _so_, _too_, _as_, etc.). He assigned subordinating conjunctions the status of prepositions, along with sentential complements, but he was unable to find a place for complementizers and co-ordinating conjunctions even in his extended system.

Aronoff's notion of "major lexical category" does not fit well into this system of Jackendoff's. On the one hand, prepositions constitute a major lexical category within Jackendoff's system but Aronoff (1976), so far as I can determine, does not have WFRs either applying to or forming prepositions. On the other hand, adverbs constitute a minor lexical category within Jackendoff's system but Aronoff (1976:92) has a WFR that takes adverbs as bases (adding the comparative suffix -er to them) and also a WFR that forms adverbs (by adding the suffix -ly to adjectives).

In discussing the types of new words that may be coined, Aronoff (1976:19-20) uses the expression "major lexical category" in such a way that it may be construed as being interchangeable with the term "open lexical category". Thus he remarks that "The only classes of words to which new words can be added by coining are major lexical categories: Noun (N), adjective (Adj), verb (V), adverb (Adv). New coinings may not be added to the various 'grammatical' categories: pronoun, determiner, quantifier, preposition, particle, modal auxiliary, etc." One may construe these remarks as signifying that Aronoff's expressions "major lexical categories" and "'grammatical' categories" denote open and closed lexical categories respectively. Aronoff (1976:20, n. 13), however, asks his readers to "Note that the latter, grammatical, categories are not closed. They may acquire new members, but by a sort of drift." If "the sort of drift" referred to by Aronoff is taken to represent a diachronic process, the note quoted above does not indicate that his notion "closed" differs from the notion "closed" that is involved in the Open Category Constraint. I return to the status of this constraint within lexicalist morphology in §2.11 below.

The Open Category Constraint is more general than the formulation (30) suggests. Specifically, as formulated in (30) it appears to be a rule-specific constraint, applicable to the formation rule (2) only. As is clear from Kempen's (1969) study, however, Afrikaans affixation rules are also subject to the Open Category Constraint. And the productive compounding rules of Afrikaans only take bases from open lexical categories as heads of new compounds. The Open Category Constraint may therefore be reformulated independently of specific Afrikaans WFRs and types of WFRs.

(39) Afrikaans WFRs of all major types apply
(a) to words of all open lexical categories, and
(b) to words of open lexical categories only.

The claims expressed by (39) are readily refutable. That is, given a descriptively adequate analysis of Afrikaans word formation on which either (39)(a) or (39)(b) is violated by one or more WFRs of <u>any</u> of the major types - compounding, affixation or reduplication - each such WFR could constitute a counterexample to (39). For example, if all the compounding and reduplication rules of such an analysis obeyed (39) but some of its affixation rules violated either (39)(a) or (39(b), the generalized constraint would clearly be incorrect. In short, the Open Category Constraint (39) is no self-confirming hypothesis, immune to refutation. This would have been the case, to be sure, had the notion of "open lexical category" been so defined as to allow every major type of WFR to select its own set of open categories.

Note that in listing the major types of WFRs to which the Open Category Constraint applies no explicit reference was made to rules of zero affixation, conversion or lexical redundancy. From studies by Kempen (1969) and Theron (1974) it is clear that Afrikaans makes extensive use of the "same" words as members of different lexical categories. What is less clear from these studies, however, is whether a given instance of such "multifunctionality" - as they call it - should be accounted for by means of rules of zero affixation, directional conversion, or lexical redundancy.[16]

Neither Kempen's nor Theron's analysis of the lexical "multifunctionality" of Afrikaans words is presented within a theoretical framework that provides a clear and principled distinction between zero affixation, directional conversion and non-directional lexical redundancy. So, without reanalyzing their data in detail, it is difficult to bring their claims about "multifunctionality" in Afrikaans to bear on the Open Category Constraint.

It is not highly plausible that all the cases of "directional multifunctionality" - i.e., cases in which a word is a member of one lexical category primarily and a member of one or more other lexical categories secondarily only - that they claim to exist have to be accounted for by rules of zero affixation and/or rules of directional conversion. Even if one were to make this implausible assumption, however, the Open Category Constraint would not be undermined by the rules of zero affixation and/or conversion required for this account.

Theron's study - which is the more detailed of the two - yields one potentially problematic case. She (1974:291) presents data which could be accounted for by rules of zero affixation or conversion that take (what she calls) interjections as bases for the formation of adverbs and verbs. The following sets of sentences illustrate the point: in the (a) sentences the interjection is underscored, in the (b) sentences the corresponding adverbs, and in the (c) sentences the corresponding verbs.

(40) (a) Hy val in die water: "Pardoems"!
he fall into the water 'splash'
"He falls into the water with a splash."
(b) Hy val pardoems in die water.
he fall 'splash' into the water
"He falls splashing int the water."
(c) Hy pardoems in die water in.
he splash into the water in
"He splashes into the water."
(41) (a) "Woerts!" Jaag hy om die hoek.
'whiz' tear he around the corner
"Whiz! He nips around the corner."
(b) Hy jaag woerts om die hoek.
he tear 'whiz' around the corner
"He goes whizzing around the corner."

(c) Hy woerts om die hoek.
he whiz around the corner
"He whizzes around the corner."

As was noted above, however, the status of interjections is problematic within the framework of the lexical categories adopted by lexicalist syntacticians and morphologists. Consequently, it is not clear that such general conditions on WFRs as the Open Category Constraint should apply to the rules of zero affixation/conversion under consideration, even if the postulation of these rules were justifiable at all.

Formulated as (39), then, the Open Category Constraint is independent of specific Afrikaans WFRs and types of WFRs. That is, the constraint is rule (-type) independent. It is to be hoped that the constraint will turn out to be in some clear sense language-independent as well. An investigation of the latter aspect of the constraint would, however, go well beyond the restricted scope of the present study.

It is possible to reduce the set of open lexical categories in Afrikaans by taking numerals to be nouns rather than quantifiers. The argument for assigning numerals the status of nouns, specifically group nouns, is parallel to the one that Jackendoff (1977:128-30) has used to justify a similar category reanalysis for English. This argument is based on the specifier system. Numerals (e.g., twee (= "two"), tien (= "ten")) are like group nouns (e.g., dosyn (= "dozen"), aantal (= "number")) in that they cannot be preceded by degree words such as te (= "too"), hoe (= "how"), verskriklik/ontsettend (= "terribly"), and ongelooflik (= "unbelievably"), whereas quantifiers such as baie/veel (= "many") and min (= "few"/ "little") can.

(42) (a) $*\begin{Bmatrix}\text{te}\\ \text{hoe}\end{Bmatrix}\begin{Bmatrix}\text{twee}\\ \text{tien}\end{Bmatrix}$ (b) $*\begin{Bmatrix}\text{te}\\ \text{hoe}\end{Bmatrix}\begin{Bmatrix}\text{dosyn}\\ \text{aantal}\end{Bmatrix}$ (c) $\begin{Bmatrix}\text{te}\\ \text{hoe}\end{Bmatrix}\begin{Bmatrix}\text{baie}\\ \text{min}\end{Bmatrix}$

Like nouns, numerals can be preceded by adjectives and the indefinite article.

(43) (a) 'n mooi twee weke
a beautiful two weeks
"a beautiful two weeks"

'n stowwerige vier myl (van die pad)
a dusty four mile (of the road)
"a dusty four miles"
'n hele sewentien bladsye
a whole seventeen pages
"a whole seventeen pages"

(b) 'n geweldige aantal mense
a tremendous number people
"a tremendous number of people"
'n nuttelose paar dae
a useless couple days
"a useless couple of days"
'n hele tros piesangs
a whole bunch bananas
"a whole bunch of bananas"

Numerals, moreover, function like nouns in partitives.

(44) (a) die mooiste twee van daardie weke
the beautiful SUPERL two of those weeks
"the most beautiful two of those weeks"
'n stowwerige vier van die baie myle grondpad
a dusty four of the many miles dust road
"four dusty miles of the many miles of dirt road"
'n hele sewentien van die getikte bladsye
a whole seventeen of the typed pages
"a whole seventeen of the typed pages"

(b) 'n geweldige aantal van die mense
a tremendous number of the people
"a tremendous number of the people"
'n nuttelose paar van die oorblywende dae
a useless few of the remaining days
"a useless few of the remaining days"
'n hele tros van die vrot piesangs
a whole bunch of the rotten bananas
"a whole bunch of the rotten bananas"

Assigning numerals the status of nouns makes it possible to say that Afrikaans has only four open lexical categories: Noun, Verb, Adjective, Adverb.

To sum up: the formation rule (2), if it is made subject to the Open Category Constraint (39) - which has to be postulated anyway - need not stipulate the lexical category of the bases of Afrikaans reduplications.

2.6 Lexical category of reduplications

The rule of reduplication (2) does not stipulate the lexical category of the reduplications it forms. Theories of lexicalist morphology typically attempt to specify the lexical category of newly formed words by means of rule-independent devices. Allen (1978:105ff.), for example, formulates for this purpose what she calls the "Is A Condition", which states, amongst other things, that the syntactic category of a word formed by a WFR is that of the right-hand constituent of the word. Williams (1981), Lieber (1981) and Selkirk (1982) use "percolation" devices for the same purpose. In terms of these the category specification of the head - normally in English the right-hand constituent of a complex word - is assigned to the word as a whole. And recently Kiparsky (1982:6) also with this end in view has formulated a constraint whose gist is "that word formation is endocentric". Kiparsky fleshes out this constraint, which may be called the "Endocentricity Constraint", as follows:

(45) The category of a derived word is always non-distinct from the category of its head.[17]

Given the Endocentricity Constraint - or one of the other functionally related devices mentioned above - individual WFRs need not stipulate the lexical category of the output words. For the purpose of the present discussion, it is not necessary to determine which of the devices proposed in the literature is most adequate. Kiparsky's general formulation of the constraint in question will do if we take the expression "head" to denote the (nonreduplicated) base in the case of Afrikaans reduplications.

Recall that in terms of the Open Category Constraint the bases to which the Afrikaans formation rule (2) applies may be nouns (including cardinals), verbs, adjectives or adverbs.

Given the Endocentricity Constraints, the following prediction may be made:

(46) The formation rule (2) will copy nouns, verbs, adjectives and adverbs to form noun, verb, adjective and adverb reduplications respectively.

It should of course be kept in mind that the category Noun, in keeping with the conclusion drawn in §2.5 above, is taken here to include numerals, specifically cardinals.

The essence of the predictions of (46) is that Afrikaans does not have exocentric reduplications. At first glance, this claim appears to be false: in Chapter 1 it was noted that, on conventional analyses, reduplication creates a diversity of exocentric forms in Afrikaans. It is therefore necessary to consider in some detail the various types of exocentric reduplications that have been postulated by conventional analyses. Because of its comprehensive scope, I will concentrate on Kempen's (1969) study, though other studies such as those by Scholtz (1963), Botha (1964), Raidt (1981), and Hauptfleisch (in preparation) also make provision, explicitly or implicitly, for a variety of types of exocentric Afrikaans reduplications. On conventional analyses, then, the following types of exocentric reduplications may be productively formed in Afrikaans.

A Verbs formed by the reduplication of nouns

<table>
<tr><td>(47)</td><td>(a)</td><td>Sy</td><td><u>kruk - kruk</u></td><td>stadig</td><td>oor</td><td>die</td><td>woelige</td><td>straat.</td></tr>
<tr><td></td><td></td><td>she</td><td>crutch crutch</td><td>slowly</td><td>across</td><td>the</td><td>busy</td><td>street</td></tr>
</table>

"She moves slowly across the busy street on her crutches."

<table>
<tr><td>(b)</td><td>Die</td><td>kinders</td><td><u>bobbejaan-bobbejaan</u></td><td>rats</td><td>teen</td></tr>
<tr><td></td><td>the</td><td>children</td><td>monkey monkey</td><td>agile</td><td>against</td></tr>
<tr><td></td><td>die</td><td>hang</td><td>op.</td><td></td><td></td></tr>
<tr><td></td><td>the</td><td>slope</td><td>up</td><td></td><td></td></tr>
</table>

"The children are scaling the slope with monkey-like agility."

(c) Stertswaaiend neus-neus Rex die bal nader.
tail wagging nose nose Rex the ball closer
"Wagging his tail, Rex nudges the ball closer with his nose."

B *Adverbs formed by the reduplication of nouns*

(48) (a) Die pad was ent - ent sleg.
the road was stretch stretch bad
"The road was bad in some (scattered) stretches."

(b) Die skape wei troppe-troppe op die vlakte.
the sheep graze flocks flocks on the plain
"The sheep are grazing on the plain in (several) scattered flocks."

(c) Hy loop stywebeen - stywebeen die straat af.
he walk stiff + leg stiff + leg the street down
[= (23)(b)]
"He goes down the street, his leg(s) as stiff as anything."

(d) Hulle kies witpens - witpens die koers
they choose white+belly white+belly the direction
na die oop see.
to the open sea
"They head for the open sea, showing their white bellies (= sails)."

C *Nouns formed by the reduplication of verbs*

(49) (a) Die kinders speel vang - vang.
the children play catch catch
"The children are playing at catch-me-if-you-can."

(b) Ek is nou moeg van raai - raai speel.
I am now tired of guess guess play
"I am now tired of playing at riddles."

(c) Van soek - soek sal hulle nooit moeg word nie.
of search search will they never tired become not
"They will never grow tired of the game in which the players take turns at looking for some person or thing."

D Adverbs formed by the reduplication of verbs

(50) (a) Die leeu loop brul- brul weg.
the lion walk roar roar away
"Roaring repeatedly, the lion walks away."

(b) Hy loop sing-sing in die gang af.
he walks sing sing in the corridor down
"Singing merrily, he goes down the passage."

(c) Sy doen die werk huil-huil.
she do the work cry cry
"She does the work even as she cries."

E Nouns formed by the reduplication of numerals

(51) (a) Drie - drie storm deur die hek.
three three charge through the gate
"Groups of three are charging through the gate."

(b) Tien-tien verlaat die kamer.
ten ten leave the room
"People are leaving the room, ten at a time."

(c) Vyf - vyf kom om afskeid te neem.
five five come to leave to take
"They are coming to take their leave in groups of five."

F Adverbs formed by the reduplication of numerals

(52) (a) Die bulle storm drie - drie deur die hek.
the bulls charge three three through the gate
"The bulls are charging through the gate three at a time."

(b) Die kinders verlaat tien-tien die kamer.
the children leave ten ten the room
"The children are leaving the room in groups of ten."

(c) Sy ondersteuners kom vyf - vyf om afskeid te
his supporters come five five to leave to
neem.
take
"His supporters are coming to take their leave in groups of five."

In keeping with the Galilean style - cf. specifically (2)(d) in §1 above - one would not be inclined either immediately to give up the Endocentricity Constraint (45) or to replace the rule of formation (2) by a more complex one. Because of their unifying nature, I would rather like to retain both the former constraint and the latter rule in a maximally general form. What I will do is to question the so-called facts that seem to bear negatively on this constraint and rule. Specifically, I will argue below that none of the types of forms A-F embodies any real threat to the prediction (46). There are two reasons why these forms fail to undermine the claim that Afrikaans has no exocentric reduplications. On the one hand, the postulation of every one of these types of exocentric reduplication is based on assumptions that are either unjustified or highly questionable. On the other hand, for each type there is at least one plausible analysis that does not assign it the status of exocentric reduplication.[18]

2.6.1 "Noun-based verb reduplications"

Kempen (1969:246) presents no more than two examples of forms that have the status of "noun-based verb reduplications". He remarks that "this type still occurs too infrequently for more to be said about it". But this remark clearly applies only to Kempen's own corpus of data. For it is possible to form new "noun-based verb reduplications" such as (47)(a)-(c). The forms underscored in (53) may serve to illustrate the point.

(53) (a) Rooibokke <u>string-string</u> tussen die bome deur
impalas string string among the trees through
na die watergat toe.
to the waterhole to
"Through the trees, strings of impalas are making for the water hole."

(b) 'n Valk <u>wiel - wiel</u> hoog bo die bome.
a hawk wheel wheel high above the trees
"High above the trees, a hawk is sailing round and round."

(c) Moeisaam pantoffel-pantoffel hy in die
laboriously slipper slipper he in the
hospitaalgang af.
hospital corridor down
"Padding laboriously on slippered feet, he makes his way down the hospital corridor."

(d) Die rook wolk - wolk by die skoorsteen uit.
the smoke cloud cloud at the chimney out
"Puffs of smoke are coming from the chimney."

(e) Die wind werwel-werwel oor die vlakte.
the wind swivel swivel over the plain
"The wind whirls across the plain."

Forms such as (47)(a)-(c) and (53)(a)-(e) illustrate a morphological process that cannot be said to be nonproductive. At the same time, however, such forms do not represent exocentric "noun-based verb reduplications". Rather, they should be analyzed as endocentric verb-based verb reduplications.

Observe that the base of each of the verb reduplications in (47)(a)-(c) and (53)(a)-(e) may be used unreduplicated as a verb too:

(54) (a) Sy kruk stadig oor die woelige straat.
she crutch slowly across the busy street

(b) Die kinders bobbejaan rats teen die hang op.
the children monkey agile against the slope up

(c) Stertswaaiend neus Rex die bal nader.
tail wagging nose Rex the ball closer

(d) Rooibokke string tussen die bome deur na
impalas string among the trees through to
die watergat toe.
the water hole to

(e) 'n Valk wiel hoog bo die bome.
a hawk wheel high above the trees

(f) Moeisaam pantoffel hy in die hospitaalgang
laboriously slipper he in the hospital corridor
af.
down

(g) Die rook <u>wolk</u> by die skoorsteen uit.
the smoke cloud at the chimney out

(h) Die wind <u>werwel</u> oor die vlakte.
the wind swivel over the plain

Given the availability of the verbs underscored in (54), there is no formal reason for claiming that the reduplications in (47)(a)-(c) and (53)(a)-(h) are based on the nouns <u>kruk</u> (= "crutch"), <u>bobbejaan</u> (= "monkey"), <u>neus</u> (= "nose"), <u>string</u> (= "string"), <u>wiel</u> (= "wheel"), <u>pantoffel</u> (= "slipper"), <u>wolk</u> (= "cloud"), and <u>werwel</u> (= "swivel") respectively. Kempen's (1969:246) analysis provides no justification whatever for the claim that the nouns rather than the corresponding verbs constitute the bases for the reduplications under consideration.

Afrikaans possesses numerous lexical items that are members both of the category Verb and the category Noun, as is clear from work by Kempen (1969:34ff.) and Theron (1974:163). The question of how the relationship between such verbs and nouns is to be accounted for, however, is distinct from the question of the category status of the bases of the reduplications <u>kruk-kruk</u>, <u>bobbejaan-bobbejaan</u>, etc. The only relevant point here is that items such as <u>kruk</u>, <u>bobbejaan</u>, etc. are available as verbs to the formation rule (2). The claim, then, that Afrikaans has "noun-based verb reduplications" such as <u>kruk-kruk</u>, <u>bobbejaan-bobbejaan</u>, etc. can be accepted only if supported by strong empirical evidence. No such evidence, however, has been presented.

2.6.2 *"Noun-based adverb reduplications"*

Let us consider next an analysis of forms such as <u>ent-ent</u> (= "stretch stretch") in (48)(a), <u>troppe-troppe</u> (= "flocks flocks") in (48)(b), <u>stywebeen-stywebeen</u> (= "stiff + leg stiff + leg") in (48)(c) on which these are denied the status of exocentric "noun-based adverb reduplications". To begin with, it is necessary to draw a distinction between, on the one hand, forms such as <u>ent-ent</u> and <u>troppe-troppe</u> in which a measure or a group noun is reduplicated and, on the other hand, forms such as <u>stywebeen-stywebeen</u> and <u>witpens-witpens</u> (=

"white + belly white + belly") in which the reduplicated noun is not a measure or a group noun.

We consider first a plausible endocentric analysis of the measure/group noun subtype. On this analysis the Afrikaans formation rule (2) applies freely both to the singular and to the plural forms of all nouns, including measure and group nouns, to yield reduplications such as ent-ent/ente-ente, kol-kol/kolle-kolle, lap-lap/lappe-lappe, plek-plek/plekke-plekke, stuk-stuk/stukke-stukke. In accordance with the Endocentricity Constraint these reduplications are, of course, nouns.

As (constituents of) measure phrases, measure/group nouns may occur in various positions in Afrikaans sentences. This claim may be illustrated with reference to the items ent, kol, stuk and lap for three such sentential positions. In (55)-(58) these items are shown to occur in a head position (in the (a) sentences), in a prehead position (in the (b) sentences), and in a predicate position after the (auxiliary) verb (in the (c) sentences).

(55) (a) 'n Ent het ingestort.
a stretch has collapsed
"A stretch collapsed."

(b) 'n Ent muur het ingestort.
a stretch wall has collapsed
"A stretch of (the) wall collapsed."

(c) Die muur het 'n ent ingestort.
the wall has a stretch collapsed
"A portion of the wall collapsed."

(56) (a) Kolle het verdroog.
patches have withered
"Patches have withered."

(b) Kolle gras het verdroog.
patches grass have withered
"Patches of grass have withered."

(c) Die gras het kolle verdroog.
the grass has patches withered
"The grass has withered in patches."

(57) (a) 'n <u>Stuk</u> het weg gespoel.
a stretch has away washed
"A stretch was washed away."

(b) 'n <u>Stuk</u> pad het weg gespoel.
a stretch road has away washed
"A stretch of road was washed away."

(c) Die pad het 'n <u>stuk</u> weg gespoel.
the road has a stretch away washed
"A section of the road was washed away."

(58) (a) <u>Lappe</u> staan onder water.
patches stand under water
"Patches are under water."

(b) <u>Lappe</u> aartappels staan onder water.
patches potatoes stand under water
"Patches of potatoes are under water."

(c) Die aartappels staan <u>lappe</u> onder water.
the potatoes stand patches under water
"The potatoes are under water in patches."

In the (c) sentences above, the measure/group nouns occur in a position where adverbs can appear too.

(59) (a) Die muur het <u>dramaties</u> ingestort.
the wall has dramatically collapsed
"The wall collapsed dramatically."

(b) Die gras het <u>vinnig</u> verdroog.
the grass has fast withered
"The grass has withered fast."

(c) Die pad het <u>heeltemal</u> weg gespoel.
the road has completely away washed
"The road was washed away completely."

(d) Die aartappels staan <u>lank</u> onder water.
the potatoes stand long under water
"The potatoes have been under water for a long time."

The measure/group nouns in the (c) sentences of (55)-(58) have the category status of Noun, however, as is indicated by the (singular) indefinite articles and plural forms.

Neither the fact that they occur in a position where adverbs can also occur, nor the fact that the noun phrases of which they are constituents are within the verb phrase, indicates that ent, kolle, stuk and lappe have the category status of Adverb.

The fact that a measure/group noun may occur as (constituent of) a measure phrase in three (or more) different sentential positions is not stated in the lexical entry of the noun. Rather, a lexical redundancy rule will state this fact as part of a generalization covering all measure/group nouns.[19] This rule expresses the claim that it is less costly for the grammar of Afrikaans to have measure/group nouns that occur in all three (or more) positions than to have measure/group nouns that occur in some of these positions only. As has been noted by Wasow (1977:330), the lexicon is generally taken to be "... the receptacle of idiosyncratic information about the elements of the vocabulary of a language". Since lexical redundancy rules are devices within the lexicon it is "... natural that [they] should be conceived of as freely allowing unsystematic exceptions", to use Wasow's formulation (1977: 330) once more.[20] One would therefore expect the lexical redundancy rule specifying the various positions in which measure/group nouns may occur to have exceptions that are idiosyncratic from a formal point of view.[21] And this is in fact the case. There are measure/group nouns that cannot appear in both the singular and plural form in all positions and there are group nouns that can appear in neither the singular nor the plural form in certain positions.

(60) (a) Die gras het kolle verdroog. [= (56)(c)]
the grass has patches withered

(b) *Die gras het 'n kol verdroog.
the grass has a patch withered
"*The grass has withered in a patch."

(61) (a) Die aartappels staan lappe onder water.
the potatoes stand patches under water
[= (58)(c)]

(b) *Die aartappels staan 'n lap onder water.
the potatoes stand a patch under water

(62) (a) 'n <u>Plek</u> het weg gespoel.
a place has away washed
"A place washed away."

(b) <u>Plekke</u> het weg gespoel.
places have away washed
"Places washed away."

(c) *'n <u>Plek</u> pad het weg gespoel.
a place road has away washed
"*Places of road washed away."

(d) *<u>Plekke</u> pad het weg gespoel.
places road have away washed
"*Places of road washed away."

(e) ?Die pad het 'n <u>plek</u> weg gespoel.
the road has a place away washed
"The road washed away in one place."

(f) Die pad het <u>plekke</u> weg gespoel.
the road has places away washed
"The road washed away in places."

(63) (a) 'n <u>Klompie</u> sit in die son.
a small number sit in the sun
"A handful are sitting in the sun."

(b) <u>Klompies</u> sit in die son.
small numbers sit in the sun
"Scattered small groups are sitting in the sun."

(c) 'n <u>Klompie</u> mense sit in die son.
a small number people sit in the sun
"A small party of people are sitting in the sun."

(d) <u>Klompies</u> mense sit in die son.
small numbers people sit in the sun
"People are sitting around in the sun in scattered handfuls."

(e) *Die mense sit 'n <u>klompie</u> in die son.
the people sit a small number in the sun
"*The people are sitting in the sun in a handful."

(f) *Die mense sit <u>klompies</u> in die son.
the people sit small numbers in the sun
"The people are sitting around in the sun in scattered handfuls."

If measure/group noun reduplications are formed by the formation rule (2), they will, like nonreduplicated measure/group nouns, automatically fall within the scope of the lexical redundancy rule considered above. That is, this rule will specify that it would be less costly for the grammar of Afrikaans if these reduplications were able to occur in a head position, in a prehead position, and in a predicate position after the verb. Moreover, it is to be expected that, like some nonreduplicated measure/group nouns, some measure/group noun reduplications will constitute exceptions to this rule, exceptions that are idiosyncratic from a formal point of view. Both of these expectations are borne out by data about the ability of reduplications such as <u>ent-ent</u>, <u>ente-ente</u>, <u>kol-kol</u>, <u>kolle-kolle</u>, <u>stuk-stuk</u>, <u>stukke-stukke</u>, <u>lap-lap</u>, <u>lappe-lappe</u>, <u>klompie-klompie</u>, and <u>klompies-klompies</u> to appear in a head position (in the (a) sentences below), in a prehead position (in the (b) sentences) and in a predicate position after the auxiliary verb (in the (c) sentences).

(64) (a) (i) <u>Ent - ent</u> het ingestort. (cf. (55))
stretch stretch have collapsed
"A couple of sections have collapsed."

(ii) <u>Ente - ente</u> het ingestort.
stretches stretches have collapsed
"Quite a few sections have collapsed."

(b) (i) ?<u>Ent - ent</u> muur het ingestort.
stretch stretch wall have collapsed
"A couple of sections of wall have collapsed."

(ii) <u>Ente - ente</u> muur het ingestort.
stretches stretches wall have collapsed
"Quite a few sections of wall have collapsed."

(c) (i) Die muur het <u>ent - ent</u> ingestort.
the wall has stretch stretch collapsed
"The wall has collapsed in a couple of places."

(ii) Die muur het <u>ente - ente</u> ingestort.
the wall has stretches stretches collapsed
"The wall has collapsed in quite a few places."

(65) (a) (i) <u>Kol - kol</u> het verdroog. (cf. (56))
patch patch have withered
"A couple of patches have withered."
(ii) <u>Kolle - kolle</u> het verdroog.
patches patches have withered
"Quite a few patches have withered."
(b) (i) *<u>Kol - kol</u> gras het verdroog.
patch patch grass have withered
"A couple of patches of grass have withered."
(ii) <u>Kolle - kolle</u> gras het verdroog.
patches patches grass have withered
"Quite a few patches of grass have withered."
(c) (i) Die gras het <u>kol - kol</u> verdroog.
the grass has patch patch withered
"The grass has withered in a couple of places."
(ii) Die gras het <u>kolle - kolle</u> verdroog.
the grass has patches patches withered
"The grass has withered in quite a few places."

(66) (a) (i) <u>Stuk - stuk</u> het weg gespoel. (cf. (57))
stretch stretch have away washed
"A couple of sections have washed away."
(ii) <u>Stukke - stukke</u> het weg gespoel.
stretches stretches have away washed
"Quite a few sections have washed away."
(b) (i) ?<u>Stuk - stuk</u> pad het weg gespoel.
stretch stretch road have away washed
"A couple of sections of road have washed away."
(ii) <u>Stukke - stukke</u> pad het weg gespoel.
stretches stretches road have away washed
"Quite a few sections of road have washed away."
(c) (i) Die pad het <u>stuk - stuk</u> weg gespoel.
the road has stretch stretch away washed
"The road has washed away in a couple of places."

(ii) Die pad het stukke - stukke weg gespoel.
the road has stretches stretches away washed
"The road has washed away in quite a few places."

(67) (a) (i) Lap - lap staan onder water. (cf. (58))
patch patch stand under water
"A couple of patches are under water."

(ii) Lappe - lappe staan onder water.
patches patches stand under water
"Quite a few patches are under water."

(b) (i) ?/*Lap - lap aartappels staan onder water.
patch patch potatoes stand under water
"A couple of patches of potatoes are under water."

(ii) Lappe - lappe aartappels staan onder water.
patches patches potatoes stand under water
"Quite a few patches of potatoes are under water."

(c) (i) Die aartappels staan lap - lap onder water.
the potatoes stand patch patch under water
"The potatoes are under water in a couple of places."

(ii) Die aartappels staan lappe - lappe onder
the potatoes stand patches patches under
water.
water
"The potatoes are under water in quite a few places."

(68) (a) (i)?Klompie - klompie sit in die son.
small number small number sit in the sun
"A couple of handfuls are sitting in the sun."

(ii) Klompies - klompies sit in die son.
small numbers small numbers sit in the sun
"Quite a few handfuls are sitting in the sun."

(b) (i) ?Klompie - klompie mense sit in die
small number small number people sit in the
son.
sun
"A couple of handfuls of people are sitting around in the sun."

(ii) Klompies - klompies mense sit in die
small numbers small numbers people sit in the
son.
sun
"Quite a few handfuls of people are sitting around in the sun."

(c) (i) ?Die mense sit klompie - klompie
the people sit small number small number
in die son.
in the sun
"?The people are sitting around in the sun in just a few handfuls."

(ii) Die mense sit klompies - klompies
the people sit small numbers small numbers
in die son.
in the sun
"?The people are sitting around in the sun in quite a few handfuls."

It should be noted that judgments about the acceptability of Afrikaans reduplications vary in many cases - e.g., (64)(b)(i), (66)(b)(i), (67)(b)(i), (68)(a)(i), (b)(i) and (c)(i): different speakers make different judgments about the acceptability of the same reduplications and one and the same speaker judges the acceptability of the same reduplications differently at different times.

The salient point is that, when reduplicated measure/group nouns appear in the predicate position after the (auxiliary) verb, like nonreduplicated measure/group nouns they do not exhibit the categorial properties of adverbs. For example, they cannot form bases for comparative -er suffixation, superlative -ste suffixation, -heid (= "-ness") suffixation, and -erig (= "-ishly") suffixation.[22] From the fact that such reduplications occur in a position in which adverbs can also occur, conventional studies seem to have inferred, incorrectly, that these reduplications are members of the lexical category Adverb. It is not the case, therefore, that measure/group noun reduplications, when they occur in the predicate position, instantiate an exocentric type of reduplication. When in this position, they are simply noun-based noun reduplications. The fact that ent-ent in (64)(c)(i) and stuk-stuk in (66)(c)(i), for example, cannot be accompanied by the singular indefinite article 'n (= "a") - which does occur with the unreduplicated ent in (55)(c) and stuk in (57)(c) - does not indicate that ent-ent and stuk-stuk are not nouns in the predicate position. Rather, the reason why ent-ent and stuk-stuk cannot be accompanied by the indefinite article is simply the fact that an aspect of their meaning may be characterized as "some, more than one".

We turn next to the second subtype of "noun-based adverb reduplications", the subtype exemplified by stywebeen-stywebeen (= "stiff + leg stiff + leg") in (48)(c) and witpens-witpens (= "white + belly white + belly") in (48)(d). There is a plausible analysis of such reduplications on which they are endocentric adverb reduplications formed by the copying of adverbs. Such an analysis, therefore, denies the claim that these reduplications are noun-based.

Basic to this endocentric analysis of stywebeen-stywebeen, etc. is the claim that Afrikaans has a large number of lexical items that are members of both the category Noun and the category Adverb. Kempen (1969:70ff.) and, especially, Theron (1974:201ff.) furnish numerous examples of such items, including the underscored forms in (69)-(73), which are nouns in the (a) sentences and adverbs in the (b) sentences.

(69) (a) Hy wys met sy duim.
he point with his thumb
"He points with his thumb."

(b) Hy ry duim Kaapstad toe.
he rides thumb Cape Town to
"He is hitch-hiking to Cape Town."

(70) (a) Die tou by die ingang is lank.
the queue at the entrance is long
"The queue at the entrance is long."

(b) Hulle staan tou by die ingang.
they stand queue at the entrance
"They are queuing at the entrance."

(71) (a) Ons plan is 'n geheim.
our plan is a secret
"Our plan is a secret."

(b) Ons hou die plan geheim.
we keep the plan secret
"We are keeping the plan a secret."

(72) (a) Hy is 'n grootbek.
he is a big mouth
"He is a braggart."

(b) Hy praat grootbek oor sy ervaringe.
he talk big mouth about his experiences
"He talks boastfully about his experiences."

(73) (a) Sy het 'n skeeloog.
she has a squint-eye
"She has a squint-eye."

(b) Sy staar skeeloog na die prent.
she stare squint-eye at the picture
"She stares squint-eyed at the picture."

Whether the multiple category membership of items such as those underscored in (69)-(73) is to be accounted for by a directional rule of zero affixation, by a nondirectional lexical redundancy rule or by both is immaterial to the present discussion.[23]

The items stywebeen (= "stiff leg") and witpens (= "white belly") - constituting the bases of the reduplications stywebeen-stywebeen and witpens-witpens, respectively - have the same multiple category membership as duim, tou, geheim, grootbek, skeeloog, etc.

(74) (a) Sy stywebeen sal hom uit die wedstryd hou.
his stiff leg will him out the match keep
"His stiff leg will keep him out of the match."

(b) Hy loop stywebeen die straat af.
he walk stiff leg the street down
"He walks stiff-legged/with a stiff leg down the street."

(75) (a) Hy begeer 'n witpens.
he covet a white belly
"He covets something (boat, animal, ...) with a white belly."

(b) Hulle kies witpens die koers na die oop see.
they choose white belly the direction to the open sea
"Showing a white belly, they head for the open sea."

On Kempen's and Theron's analysis, then, stywebeen and witpens are adverbs in sentences (74)(b) and (75)(b) respectively. But this entails that these items are also available as adverbs to serve as bases for the formation rule (2). Consequently, the forms stywebeen-stywebeen in (48)(d) and witpens-witpens in (48)(c) can straightforwardly be analyzed as adverb-based adverb reduplications. Any exocentric analysis of these forms will require special justification, justification not found in the conventional arguments for assigning the bases of such reduplications the status of nouns.

In sum, then: the claim that Afrikaans has exocentric "noun-based adverb reduplications" cannot be upheld. On the one hand, reduplications of the type ent-ent are nouns rather than adverbs. On the other hand, reduplications such as stywebeen-stywebeen are based on adverbs rather than on nouns.[24]

2.6.3 "Verb-based noun reduplications"

Commenting on the comprehensiveness of coverage of Kempen's (1969) analysis of Afrikaans reduplication, Hauptfleisch (in preparation:24) observes that Kempen does not describe forms such as those underscored in (49)(a)-(c) above. Though his formulation is not fully explicit, Hauptfleisch apparently considers nouns such as vang-vang (= "catch catch"), raai-raai (= "guess guess"), soek-soek (= "search search"), etc. to be reduplications formed by the copying of verbs. To do so is in effect to assign these forms the status of exocentric reduplications.

There are two alternative analyses, however, on neither of which forms such as vang-vang, raai-raai, soek-soek, etc. need be assigned the status of exocentric reduplications. The first alternative proceeds from the observation that corresponding to the nouns vang-vang, raai-raai, soek-soek, etc. there are endocentric verb reduplications.

(76) (a) Die kinders vang-vang mekaar om die beurt.
the children catch catch each other in the turn
"The children are taking it in turns catching one another"

(b) Raai - raai hoeveel besems het 'n heks?
guess guess how many brooms has a witch
"Riddle me a riddle: how many brooms has a witch?"

(c) Hulle soek - soek al die hele oggend na
they search search already the whole morning to
mekaar.
each other
"They have been looking for each other frantically all morning."

The nouns vang-vang, raai-raai, and soek-soek may be related to the corresponding verbs in (76)(a)-(c) in terms of lexical redundancy or zero affixation. Whether the rule required for this is a lexical redundancy rule or a rule of zero affixation is immaterial to this analysis. What does matter is that this analysis does not assign the nouns vang-vang, raai-raai, soek-soek, etc. the status of reduplications.

The rule that relates the nouns vang-vang, raai-raai, and soek-soek to the corresponding verbs is needed independently in the grammar of Afrikaans. As has been shown by Kempen (1969:34ff.) and Theron (1974:166ff.), Afrikaans possesses numerous lexical items that are both verbs and nouns. This point may be illustrated with reference to vang, raai and soek, which are verbs in the (a) sentences below and nouns in the (b) sentences.

(77) (a) Jan vang die bal.
John catch the ball
"John catches the ball."

(b) Vang is moeiliker as gooi.
catch is more difficult than throw
"It is more difficult to catch than to throw/
Catching is more difficult than throwing."

(78) (a) Hy raai die antwoord.
he guess the answer
"He guesses the answer."

(b) Jy kry net een raai.
you get only one guess
"You are allowed one guess only."

(79) (a) Hulle soek die moordenaars.
they search the murderers
"They are looking for the murderers."

(b) Die soek van moordenaars is gevaarlike werk.
the search of murderers is dangerous work
"Looking for murderers is dangerous work."

The rule under consideration is needed, therefore, to relate the nonreduplicated nouns in the (b) sentences above to the nonreduplicated verbs in the (a) sentences.

This brings us to the second alternative analysis on which the Afrikaans nouns vang-vang, raai-raai, soek-soek, etc. do not have the status of exocentric reduplications. From the discussion above it is clear that vang, raai and soek are also members of the category Noun. This entails that they may, as nouns, constitute bases for the formation rule (2). This rule may apply to these items to form noun-based noun reduplications. Thus, vang-vang, raai-raai, and soek-soek in (49) may also have the status of endocentric noun-based noun reduplications. Which of the two alternative endocentric analyses of these forms is to be preferred is a question that need not be settled here.[25] The salient point is that, given the availability of these two endocentric analyses, there is no need to adopt the exocentric analysis considered above. To justify this exocentric analysis its proponents would have to show some clear sense in which it was more adequate than the two endocentric analyses.

2.6.4 "Verb-based adverb reduplications"

Forms such as brul-brul (= "roar roar") in (50)(a), sing-sing (= "sing sing") in (50)(b), and huil-huil (= "cry cry") in (50)(c) have conventionally been analyzed as "verb-based adverb reduplications".[26] There are various possible analyses on which such forms are denied this exocentric status. We consider the outlines of two below.

On the first alternative the forms under consideration are analyzed as adverbs formed by the reduplication of adverbs. This analysis takes as its point of departure the position that Afrikaans has lexical items that are members of both the category Verb and the category Adverb. Theron (1974:219ff.) considers, for example, eerbiedig (= "respect"), gehoorsaam (= "obey") and matig (= "moderate") as items that are both verbs (in the (a) sentences below) and adverbs (in the (b) sentences).

(80) (a) Hy eerbiedig sy ouers se wense.
he respect his parents' wishes
"He respects the wishes of his parents."

(b) Hy luister eerbiedig na sy ouers se wense.
he listen respectfully to his parents' wishes
"He listens respectfully to the wishes of his parents."

(81) (a) Die soldate gehoorsaam die bevel.
the soldiers obey the command
"The soldiers obey the command."

(b) Die soldate voer gehoorsaam die bevel uit.
the soldiers execute obediently the command out
"The soldiers execute the command obediently."

(82) (a) Hy matig sy drankgebruik.
he moderate his alcohol consumption
"He moderates his consumption of alcohol."

(b) Hy gebruik alkohol matig.
he use alcohol moderately
"He uses alcohol in moderation."

Theron (1974:220) considers the "multifunctionality" exhibited by eerbiedig, gehoorsaam, matig and the many other similar items cited by her to be "symmetrical". Within the present framework this form of multiple category membership may be accounted for by means of a nondirectional lexical redundancy rule.

The availability of such a rule means that it is possible for the bases of the reduplications brul-brul, sing-sing and huil-huil also to be assigned multiple category status. That is, given this lexical redundancy rule it would be possible for brul, sing and huil to be members of both the category Verb and the category Adverb. This, in turn, makes it possible for the former reduplications to be based not on the verbs brul, sing and huil, but rather on the adverbs brul, sing and huil. In terms of this possibility brul-brul, sing-sing and huil-huil would then be endocentric adverb-based adverb reduplications.

This analysis, however, has one particularly unattractive property. The majority of the bases of adverb reduplications such as brul-brul, sing-sing and huil-huil, etc. cannot be used unreduplicated as adverbs in Afrikaans. For example, compare the following sentences with the corresponding ones of (50).

(83) (a) *Die leeu loop brul weg. [cf. (50)(a)]
the lion walk roar away

(b) *Hy loop sing in die gang af. [cf. (50)(b)]
he walk sing in the corridor down

(c) *Sy doen die werk huil. [cf. (50)(c)]
she do the work cry

To rule out sentences such as (83)(a)-(c), the grammar of Afrikaans would, on the first analysis, have to incorporate the ad hoc stipulation that adverbs related by the above-mentioned lexical redundancy rule to corresponding verbs cannot be inserted lexically in an unreduplicated form. The ad hoc character of this stipulation is hardly more attractive than the exocentricity of the conventional analysis of forms such as brul-brul, etc.

Let us then consider the second alternative analysis that denies forms such as brul-brul, sing-sing, huil-huil, etc. the status of exocentric reduplications. On this alternative the adverbs brul-brul, sing-sing, huil-huil, etc. are not assigned the status of reduplications at all. Rather, they are viewed as words formed via zero affixation on the basis of the reduplicated verbs brul-brul, sing-sing, huil-huil, etc. The zero affix required by this analysis has properties similar to those of the phonologically non-null suffix -end (= "-ing"), though obviously lacking its phonological content. This analysis is supported by various considerations.

First, the analysis correctly predicts that corresponding to every adverb of the form brul-brul there will be a verb reduplication of the form brul-brul. This regular correspondence has been noted by Kempen (1969:341) too. Adverbs of the form brul-brul for which there were no corresponding verb reduplications would constitute a serious embarrassment for the analysis: it would be difficult to derive them in a non-ad hoc manner.

Second, the analysis is not threatened by what may be called the "directionality problem". As has been noted by Lieber (1981:127), for example, a zero affixation analysis involves directionality: one member of the pair of corresponding lexical items must be considered basic and the other derived. In many cases - e.g., English paint (N) and paint (V), German Ruf (N) and rufen (V) - it is difficult or impossible to decide in a non-arbitrary manner which member of the pair is basic and which is derived. In the zero affixation analysis of the Afrikaans forms under consideration this is no problem, however: whereas the verbs as endocentric forms constitute bases for the affixation rule, the adverbs as endocentric forms are not available as bases for the rule.

Third, the properties of a verb reduplication such as brul-brul are preserved in the lexical (i.e., non-affixal) constituent of the corresponding zero derived adverb. For example, the verb reduplication brul-brul and the non-affixal constituent brul-brul of the zero derived adverb have the same segmental phonological form, the same stress pattern, and the same meaning. And this is a consequence of the analysis under consideration: the properties of the non-affixal constituent of a derived form may not differ unpredictably from those of the base.[27] The preservation of the properties of the base in the non-affixal constituent of the derived form is an important consideration in Lieber's (1981:144-45) and Kiparsky's (1983:6ff.) motivation of zero affixation analyses.

Fourth, the zero affix need not be assigned properties which, in a well-constrained morphology, cannot be attributed to phonologically non-null affixes. Lexicalist morphologists such as Allen (1978:271ff.), Lieber (1981:144), and Kiparsky (1983:6) do not consider the postulation of zero affixes as such to be an ad hoc extension of the power of the lexicon or word formation component. Kiparsky (1983:6) even observes that "It would actually be mysterious if they did <u>not</u> exist: note that autosegmental tonology routinely encounters affixes with a tonal specification but no segmental substance." Zero affixes cannot, however, be postulated in an unconstrained manner. Specifically, as has been argued by Lieber (1981:119ff.), it is undesirable to have zero affixes with properties not characteristic of phonologically non-null affixes. For example, like phonologically non-null affixes, zero affixes should belong to unique lexical classes, should impose a unique argument structure on their output, and should not lead to the unmotivated marking of stems.

The zero affix required for the derivation of the adverbs <u>brul-brul</u>, <u>sing-sing</u>, <u>huil-huil</u>, etc. has none of the undesirable properties listed above. As was noted earlier on, its properties are in fact similar to those of the suffix -<u>end</u> that produces the so-called "present participle forms" of the verb. Corresponding to the underscored verbs in the (a) sentences below are the -<u>end</u> derived present participles of the (b) sentences.

(84) (a) Die leeu <u>brul</u> terwyl hy weg loop.
the lion roar while he away walk
"The lion roars as he walks away."

(b) Die leeu loop brullend weg.
the lion walk roaring away
"The lion walks away roaring."

(85) (a) Hy sing terwyl hy in die gang af loop.
he sing while he in the corridor down walk
"He sings as he goes down the corridor."

(b) Hy loop singend in die gang af.
he walk singing in the corridor down
"He goes down the corridor singing."

(86) (a) Sy huil terwyl sy die werk doen.
she cry while she the work do
"She cries even as she does the work."

(b) Sy doen die werk huilend.
she do the work crying
"She does the work, crying all the while."

Zero derived forms such as brul-brul in (50)(a), sing-sing in (50)(b), and huil-huil in (50)(c) share various properties with -end derived forms such as brullend in (88)(b).[28] As regards meaning, both the former and the latter forms express simultaneity. As regards syntactic distribution, zero derived forms and corresponding -end forms may occur in the same positions.

(87) (a) Die leeu loop brul-brul weg.
the lion walk roar roar away
"The lion walks away roaring."

(b) Die leeu loop brullend weg.
the lion walk roaring away
"The lion walks away roaring."

(88) (a) Brul-brul loop die leeu weg.
roar roar walk the lion away
"Roaring, the lion walks away."

(b) Brullend loop die leeu weg.
roaring walk the lion away
"Roaring, the lion walks away."

(89) (a) Die leeu bestorm die man brul-brul.
the lion charge the man roar roar
"The lion charges the man, roaring."

(b) Die leeu bestorm die man brullend.
the lion charge the man roaring
"The lion charges the man, roaring."

As regards syntactic structure, zero derived forms such as brul-brul, etc. and corresponding -end forms take the same range of complements.

(90) (a) (i) Die leeu loop brullend van woede weg.
the lion walk roaring of rage away
"The lion walks away roaring with rage."
(ii) Die leeu loop brul-brul van woede weg.
the lion walk roar roar of rage away
"The lion walks away roaring with rage."
(b) (i) *Die leeu loop brullend dat die kranse
the lion walk roaring that the cliffs
antwoord gee weg.
reply give away
"The lion walks away, roaring till the cliffs begin to echo."
(ii) *Die leeu loop brul-brul dat die kranse
the lion walk roar roar that the cliffs
antwoord gee weg.
reply give away
"The lion walks away, roaring till the cliffs begin to echo."

(91) (a) (i) Sy loop singend van geluk in die
she walk singing of happiness in the
gang af.
corridor down
"She goes down the corridor singing for joy."
(ii) Sy loop sing-sing van geluk in die
she walk sing sing of happiness in the
gang af.
corridor down
"She goes down the corridor singing for joy."

(b) (i) *Sy loop singend <u>of sy betaal word</u> in die
she walk singing if she paid were in the
gang af.
corridor down
"She goes down the corridor singing as if she were being paid for the job."

(ii) *Sy loop sing-sing <u>of sy betaal word</u> in die
she walk sing sing if she paid were in the
gang af.
corridor down
"She goes down the corridor singing as if she were paid for the job."

(92) (a) (i) Sy doen die werk huilend <u>van frustrasie</u>.
she do the work crying of frustration
"She does the work while crying with frustration."

(ii) Sy doen die werk huil-huil <u>van frustrasie</u>.
she do the work cry cry of frustration
"She does the work while crying with frustration."

(b) (i) *Sy doen die werk huilend <u>sonder ophou</u>.
she do the work crying without stopping
"She does the work while crying incessantly."

(ii) *Sy doen die werk huil-huil <u>sonder ophou</u>.
she do the work cry cry without stopping
"She does the work while crying incessantly."

Compare now the sentences (90)(a) with (93)(a), (90)(b) with (93(b), (91)(a) with (94)(a), (91)(b) with (94)(b), (92)(a) with (95)(a), and (92)(b) with (95)(b).

(93) (a) Die leeu brul <u>van woede</u>.
the lion roar of rage
"The lion is roaring with rage."

(b) Die leeu brul <u>dat die kranse antwoord gee</u>.
the lion roar that the cliffs reply give
"The lion roars till the cliffs begin to echo."

(94) (a) Sy sing van geluk.
she sing of joy
"She is singing for joy."

(b) Sy sing of sy betaal word.
she sing if she paid were
"She sings as if she were being paid for the job."

(95) (a) Sy huil van frustrasie.
she cry of frustration
"She is crying with frustration."

(b) Sy huil sonder ophou.
she cry without stopping
"She cries incessantly."

From this comparison it is clear that -end and the zero affix affect the complement structure of the base verb in the same way: for example, the derived form (huilend, huil-huil) retains the possibility of taking complements of the van type, but loses the possibility of taking complements of the dat, of and sonder types.

Zero derived forms and -end forms, in fact, have more properties in common than just those considered above. It will be shown below that these two sets of forms differ in parallel ways from manner adverbs that can occur in the same sentential positions, a parallelism indicative of a further range of shared properties.

Fifth, the analysis accounts for the fact that forms such as brul-brul, as opposed to their unreduplicated bases, can be used as adverbs. Consider the underscored forms in the following sentences.

(96) (a) Die leeu brul terwyl hy weg loop. [= (84)(a)]
the lion roar while he away walk

(b) Die leeu loop brul-brul weg. [= (87)(a)]
the lion walk roar roar away

(c) Die leeu loop brullend weg [= (87)(b)]
the lion walk roaring away

(d) *Die leeu loop brul weg. [= (83)(a)]
the lion walk roar away

(e) *Die leeu loop brul-brullend weg.
the lion walk roar roaring away

On the present analysis the unacceptability of (96)(d) and (e) - which characterizes numerous other forms of the same type - can be explained on the assumption that -end and the zero affix are in complementary distribution. Like #ness and +ity in English, these Afrikaans affixes apply to bases that belong to the same lexical category but that differ in regard to their morphological class or type.[29] Whereas the zero affix attaches to verb reduplications, as in (96)(b), -end attaches to unreduplicated verbs, as in (96)(c). The unacceptability of (96)(d) results from the attachment of the zero affix to an unreduplicated verb; the unacceptability of (96)(e) from the attachment of -end to a verb reduplication. Note that the restriction on the attachment of -end may represent a special case of a general constraint which in one of its versions reads as follows:

(97) An affix cannot be added to a base that already carries features associated with the affix.

Associated with -end is the semantic feature "simultaneity", but zero derived forms such as brul-brul already carry this feature. As Kiparsky (1983:11) notes, the constraint (97) was formulated by Marantz (1981) in a stronger form as a blocking principle stating that an affix cannot be added to a stem which already carries all the features of the affix. I will return to these two constraints in §2.8 and will consider a related one in Chapter 4.

The question that now arises is whether the zero affix under consideration and -end should be regarded as two distinct affixes or as two allomorphs of the same affix. There are differences between the properties of the two affixes that would be incompatible with the position that they simply represented allomorphs of the same affix. Let us consider two of these.

On the one hand, whereas -end (= derived) forms may constitute bases for a rule of -e suffixation that forms attributive adjectives, zero derived forms cannot.

(98) (a) Die leeu loop brullend weg. [= (96)(c)]
the lion walk roaring away
(b) *Die brullend leeu loop weg.
the roaring lion walk away
"The roaring lion walks away."
(c) Die brullend + E leeu loop weg.
the roaring AFFIX lion walk away
"The roaring lion walks away."

(99) (a) Die leeu loop brul-brul weg. [= (87)(a)]
the lion walk roar roar away
(b) *Die brul-brul leeu loop weg.
the roar roar lion walk away
(c) *Die [brul-brul] + E leeu loop weg.
the roar roar AFFIX lion walk away

The point is illustrated by singend and sing-sing, huilend and huil-huil and numerous other pairs of -end and corresponding zero derived forms. In short: -end suffixation potentiates -e suffixation, but the zero affixation rule under consideration does not.

On the other hand, -end forms such as brullend differ from zero derived forms such as brul-brul syntactically as well. That is, the -end forms can take an adverbial modifier of manner, but the other forms cannot.

(100) (a) Die leeu loop luid brullend weg.
the lion walk loud roaring away
"The lion walks away roaring loudly."
(b) *Die leeu loop luid brul-brul weg.
the lion walk loud roar roar away

(101) (a) Hy loop vrolik singend in die gang af.
he walk cheerfully singing in the corridor down
"He goes down the corridor singing merrily."
(b) *Hy loop vrolik sing-sing in die gang af.
he walk cheerfully singing in the corridor down

(102) (a) Sy doen die werk sag huilend.
she do the work softly crying
"She does the work, crying softly all the while."

(b) *Sy doen die werk sag huil-huil.
she do the work softly cry cry

Returning to the main point, we may observe that the differences between -end forms and the corresponding zero derived forms do not follow from the claim that -end and the zero affix represent different allomorphs of one and the same affix. Since these differences also do not appear to be related to the difference in morphological structure between the bases - unreduplicated vs. reduplicated - they can best be accounted for by considering -end and the zero affix to represent related but distinct affixes.

The similarities between the properties of -end on the one hand and those of the zero affix on the other hand give rise to an interesting question about the (lexical) category status of zero derived forms such as brul-brul, sing-sing, huil-huil, etc. To be able to formulate this question, we have to consider the category status of the corresponding -end forms, namely brullend, singend, huilend, etc. Conventionally these -end forms have been viewed as present participles - in other words as forms of the verb. That is, -end forms have in fact been assigned the category status of verbs, not that of adverbs. This analysis is supported by the differences between -end forms and manner adverbs that occur in the same sentential positions. Some of these differences are illustrated by the following pairs of sentences, the (a) sentence containing stadig (= "slowly"), a typical manner adverb, and the (b) sentence brullend, a typical -end form.

(103) (a) Die leeu loop stadig + ER weg (as die buffel).
the lion walk slowly -er away (than the buffalo)
"The lion walks away slower than the buffalo."

(b) *Die leeu loop brullend + ER weg (as die
the lion walk roaring + er away (than the
buffel).
buffalo)
"*The lion walks away more roaring (than the
buffalo)."

(104) (a) Die leeu loop die <u>stadig + STE</u> weg.
the lion walk the slowly -est away
"The lion walks slowest of all away."

(b) *Die leeu loop die <u>brullend + STE</u> weg.
the lion walk the roaring -est away
"*The lion walks away most roaring of all."

(105) (a) Die leeu loop <u>stadig + RIG</u> weg.
the lion walk slowly -ish away
"The lion walks away somewhat slowly."

(b) *Die leeu loop <u>brullend + ERIG</u> weg.
the lion walk roaring -ish away
"*The lion walks away roaringish."

(106) (a) Die <u>stadig + HEID</u> waarmee die leeu wegloop,
the slowly -ness which with the lion away walk
verbaas hom.
amaze him
"The slowness with which the lion walks away surprises him."

(b) *Die <u>brullend + HEID</u> waarmee die leeu wegloop,
the roaring -ness which with the lion away walk
verbaas hom.
surprise him
"*The roaringness with which the lion walks away surprises him."

(107) (a) Die leeu loop <u>baie stadig</u> weg.
the lion walk very slowly away
"The lion walks away very slowly."

(b) *Die leeu loop <u>baie brullend</u> weg.
the lion walk very roaring away
"*The lion walks away very roaring."

(108) (a) Die leeu loop <u>te stadig na my smaak</u> weg.
the lion walk too slowly after my taste away
"The lion is walking away too slowly for my taste."

(b) *Die leeu loop <u>te brullend na my smaak</u> weg.
the lion walk too roaring after my taste away
"*The lion is walking away too roaring for my taste."

From (103) and (104) it is clear that, whereas stadig can take the comparative (-er) and superlative (-ste) suffixes, brullend cannot. Moreover, unlike stadig, brullend can constitute a base for neither -(e)rig suffixation nor -heid suffixation, as is shown by (105) and (106). And (107) and (108) indicate that brullend cannot take the types of specifiers and complements that stadig takes. Note, in addition, that stadig, in turn, cannot take the types of specifiers and complements that occur with brullend, singend and huilend.

(109) (a) *Die leeu loop luid stadig weg. [cf. (100)(a)]
the lion walk loud slowly away
"*The lion is walking away loudly slowly."
(b) *Die leeu loop stadig van woede weg.[cf. (90)(a)(i)]
the lion walk slowly of rage away
"*The lion is walking away slowly with rage."

The specifiers and complements of forms such as stadig are those typically associated with manner adverbs; those of forms such as brullend are typically associated with verbs (cf. (93)(a), (94)(a), (95)(a)). The -end forms under consideration should therefore be assigned the category status Verb rather than Adverb, as predicted by the Endocentricity Constraint (45).[30]

This brings us to the question of the category status of zero derived forms such as brul-brul. Given the similarities between -end forms such as brullend and zero derived forms such as brul-brul, the question is: Why should the latter be assigned the status of adverbs if the former have the status of verbs? Significantly, the claim that brul-brul, etc. are adverbs is not justified in conventional studies. So let us compare the properties of brul-brul - which on conventional analyses such as Kempen's (1969:341) expresses "manner" - with those of the manner adverb stadig that may occur in the same positions in a sentence. Specifically, compare the following sentences with the corresponding ones in (103)-(108).

(110) (a) *Die leeu loop [brul-brul] + ER weg (as
the lion walk roar roar -er away (than
die buffel). [cf. (103)(a)]
the buffalo)

(b) *Die leeu loop die [brul-brul] + STE weg. [cf. (104)(a)]
the lion walk the roar roar -est away

(c) *Die leeu loop [brul-brul] + ERIG weg. [cf. (105)(a)]
the lion walk roar roar -ish away

(d) *Die [brul-brul] + HEID waarmee die leeu weg-
the roar roar -ness which with the lion away
loop, verbaas hom. [cf. (106)(a)]
walk amaze him

(e) *Die leeu loop baie brul-brul weg. [cf. (107)(a)]
the lion walk very roar roar away

(f) *Die leeu loop te brul-brul na my smaak weg. [cf. (108)(a)]
the lion walk too roar roar after my taste away

Zero derived brul-brul clearly does not have the properties of a typical manner adverb such as stadig. Rather, zero derived brul-brul has the same properties as the present participle brullend, as is clear from a comparison of the sentences (110)(a)-(f) with (103)(b)-(108)(b) respectively. Items such as brul-brul and items such as stadig may occur in the same positions in sentences. This does not warrant the assignment of adverb status to the brul-brul type forms, however. Since zero derived brul-brul, huil-huil, sing-sing, etc. are similar in their formal properties to the present participles brullend, huilend, singend, etc., the natural assumption is that these zero derived forms should also have verb status. As is clear from (100)-(102) above, zero derived brul-brul, etc. have lost some of the verbal properties retained by brullend, etc. These zero derived forms have not, however, acquired new properties that are characteristic of any other lexical category, specifically of Adverb. Forms such as brul-brul in (50)(a), sing-sing in (50)(b) and huil-huil in (50)(c) therefore do not constitute "verb-based adverb reduplications".

Rather, these forms are verbs, specifically present-participle-like forms based on verb reduplications and derived from these by zero affixation.

2.6.5 "Numeral-based noun and adverb reduplications"

On conventional analyses of Afrikaans reduplication, numerals are reduplicated to form numerals,[31] nouns,[32] and adverbs.[33] Implicit in such analyses is the claim that these last two types of reduplication, exemplified by (51) and (52) above, are exocentric. There is, however, an analysis - parallel to the one presented in §2.6.2 above of so-called "noun-based adverb reduplications"- on which all numeral-based reduplications are endocentric.

First, on this endocentric analysis cardinals, such as een (= "one"), twee (= "two"), drie (= "three"), are assigned the status of nouns - a category reanalysis that was motivated in §2.5 above. An immediate consequence of this reanalysis is that drie-drie in (51)(a), tien-tien in (51)(b), and vyf-vyf in (51)(c) lose the status of exocentric "numeral-based noun reduplications" and become endocentric noun-based noun reduplications.

Second, cardinals, being nouns, constitute bases for the formation rule (2) to yield forms such as twee-twee (= "two two"), drie-drie (= "three three"), vyf-vyf (= "five five"), tien-tien (= "ten ten"), etc. In keeping with the Endocentricity Constraint (45), these forms are nouns.

Third, like reduplicated measure/group nouns, reduplicated "numerals"[34] may occur in a head position, in a pre-head position, and in a predicate position after the (auxiliary) verb. The three positions are illustrated by the (a), (b) and (c) sentences in (111)-(113) - the (i) sentences for reduplicated "numerals", the (ii) sentences for reduplicated measure/group nouns.

(111) (a) (i) Drie drie storm deur die hek. [= (51)(a)]
three three charge through the gate
(ii) Klompe-klompe storm deur die hek.
lots lots charge through the gate

(b) (i) Drie - drie bulle storm deur die hek.
three three bulls charge through the gate
(ii) Klompe-kompe bulle storm deur die hek.
lots lots bulls charge through the gate
(c) (i) Die bulle storm drie - drie deur die
the bulls charge three three through the
hek. [= (52)(a)]
gate
(ii) Die bulle storm klompe-klompe deur
the bulls charge lots lots through
die hek.
the gate

(112) (a) (i) Tien-tien verlaat die kamer. [= (51)(b)]
ten ten leave the room
(ii) Groepe-groepe verlaat die kamer.
groups groups leave the room
(b) (i) Tien-tien kinders verlaat die kamer.
ten ten children leave the room
(ii) Groepe-groepe kinders verlaat die kamer.
groups groups children leave the room
(c) (i) Die kinders verlaat tien-tien die
the children leave ten ten the
kamer. [= (52)(b)]
room
(ii) Die kinders verlaat groepe-groepe die kamer.
the children leave groups groups the room

(113) (a) (i) Vyf-vyf kom om afskeid te neem. [= (51)(c)]
five five come to leave to take
(ii) Hordes-hordes kom om afskeid te neem.
hordes hordes come for leave to take
(b) (i) Vyf-vyf ondersteuners kom om afskeid te
five five supporters come for leave to
neem.
take
(ii) Hordes-hordes ondersteuners kom om afskeid
hordes hordes supporters come for leave
te neem.
to take

(c) (i) Sy ondersteuners kom vyf - vyf om afskeid
his supporters come five five for leave
te neem. [= (52)(c)].
to take.

(ii) Sy ondersteuners kom hordes-hordes om
his supporters come hordes hordes for
afskeid te neem.
leave to take

Fourth, §2.6.2 above argued that a lexical redundancy rule is able to account for the positions in which reduplicated (as well as unreduplicated) group/measure nouns may occur in Afrikaans sentences. If (reduplicated) "numerals" were assigned the status of nouns, this rule would automatically account for the three positions in which they occurred in the (a), (b) and (c) sentences above. To use a lexical redundancy rule for this purpose would be to claim - as in the case of group/measure nouns - that the syntactic behavior of "numerals" was less than perfectly regular from a formal point of view. And the behavior of unreduplicated numerals bears out this claim. Unreduplicated "numerals" can occur in a head position and in a pre-head position; they cannot occur in a predicate position after the (auxiliary) verb.

(114) (a) Drie storm deur die hek. [cf. (111)(a)(i)]
three charge through the gate

(b) Drie bulle storm deur die hek.
three bulls charge through the gate
[cf. (111)(b)(i)]

(b) *Die bulle storm drie deur die hek.
the bulls charge three through the gate
[cf. (111)(c)(i)]

(115) (a) Tien verlaat die kamer. [cf. (112)(a)(i)
ten leave the room

(b) Tien kinders verlaat die kamer.[cf. (112)(b)(i)]
ten children leave the room

(c) *Die kinders verlaat tien die kamer.
the children leave ten the room
[cf. (112)(c)(i)]

(116) (a) Vyf kom om afskeid te neem. [cf. (113)(a)(i)
five come for leave to take

(b) Vyf ondersteuners kom om afskeid te neem.
five supporters come for leave to take
[cf. (113)(b)(i)]

(c) *Sy ondersteuners kom vyf om afskeid te neem.
his supporters come five for leave to take
[cf. (113)(c)(i)]

To return to the main point: the fact that reduplicated "numerals" can occur in three different sentential positions does not constitute proper justification for the claim that these forms belong to different lexical categories, each category associated with a particular position.[35] This claim, the basis of "exocentric" analyses of reduplicated "numerals", has not been justified by these analyses with reference to the relevant formal properties. To provide the required sort of evidence for such a claim, these formal properties have to be associated with reduplicated "numerals" in some of the three positions but not all of them. The (rudimentary) specifier system provides evidence that these properties do not vary in the various positions. For example, the specifier so (= "about", "more or less") may accompany a form such as tien-tien in all three positions.

(117) (a) So tien-tien verlaat die kamer.
about ten ten leave the room
"They are leaving the room about ten at a time."

(b) So tien-tien kinders verlaat die kamer.
about ten ten children leave the room
"About ten children at a time are leaving the room."

(c) Die kinders verlaat so tien-tien die kamer.
the children leave about ten ten the room
"The children are leaving the room about ten at a time."

Afrikaans therefore has neither "numeral-based noun reduplications" nor "numeral-based adverb reduplications". Rather, it has noun-based noun reduplications that may occur in different sentential positions.

In sum: the types of exocentric reduplications set up by conventional analyses pose no threat to the Endocentricity Constraint (45). The exocentricity of these types is apparent and not real: it reflects not some feature of Afrikaans but, rather, certain inadequacies in the framework of general linguistic and grammatical assumptions within which the conventional analyses have been presented. Specifically, this framework lacks an adequate conception of lexical redundancy and zero affixation. Moreover, it is incorrectly assumed within this framework that distinctions between lexical categories may be based solely on the fact that the items in question occur in different sentential positions.

When it comes to the relation between the lexical category of the base and that of the reduplication, the Afrikaans morphological process of reduplication is quite simple: it does not create any exocentricity.[36]

The literature contains many analyses of reduplication in languages other than Afrikaans that set up what appear to be exocentric types of reduplication.[37] It is not clear, however, that these analyses have been made within the framework of general morphological theories that incorporate well-articulated conceptions of lexical categories, of lexical redundancy, and of zero affixation. On closer investigation the exocentricity provided for by these analyses may well turn out to be an artefact of the theoretical framework within which they have been made. It is interesting to note that Lieber (1981:161), having analyzed Tagalog reduplication within the framework of an explanatory general theory of morphology, concludes that

> Rules of reduplication in Tagalog also seem to have the property that they do not, by themselves, trigger a change of category on their base forms. Reduplication rules which apply in conjunction with affixation (i.e., are triggered by affixes) may change category, but the more common state of affairs is that the lexical item derived by reduplication alone preserves the same category as its base.[38]

Given the Endocentricity Constraint (45), this "common state of affairs" is in fact the expected state of affairs and need not be specified in a grammar of Afrikaans that contains the formation rule (2).

2.7 Lexical category of constituents

In §2.4 a distinction was drawn between the bases to which the formation rule (2) applies and the constituents of the reduplications that are formed by the application of this rule to those bases. For instance, the rule (2) applies to the base ent (= "stretch") to form the reduplication ent_1-ent_2 that has the constituents ent_1 and ent_2. The same paragraph showed moreover that, whereas the bases to which the rule applies belong to the category type Word, the constituents of the resulting reduplications do not themselves have this category status. What, then, is the lexical category of these constituents? Specifically, do the individual constituents of a reduplication belong to the same lexical category as the base to which the formation rule applied to form that reduplication? Consider ent-ent, for example. Are its constituents ent_1 and ent_2 nouns like the base (word) ent? Note that the lexical category of the constituents of reduplications is not specified in the formation rule (2) itself. The question, then, is whether there are rule-independent constraints that specify the lexical category of these constituents.

Lexicalist morphologists have generally assumed that the constituents of morphologically complex words have the same (lexical) category status as the corresponding independent forms. This assumption may be formulated as the "Category Retention Constraint".

(118) The constituents of morphologically complex words retain the (lexical) category status that they have as independent forms.

Nowhere in the literature is this constraint to be found so explicitly formulated. Yet, if one examines the derived structures assigned to complex words by lexicalist morphologists, there is no doubt that these morphologists do operate with such a constraint. One need but consider the assignment of lexical categories to constituents of morphologically complex words in the following, randomly selected, cases.

(119) (a) $[+ [X]_V + ee]_N$ (Aronoff 1976:48)
where X = employ, pay ...
(b) $[[[grace]_N \# less]_A \# ness]_N$ (Allen 1978:211)
(c) $[[hard]_A [hearted]_A]_A$ (Allen 1978:255)
(d) $[counter\ _V[sign]]$ (Lieber 1981:49)
(e) N
A N
pale face (Lieber 1981:68)
(f) $_N[_N[_N[bath]_N\ _N[room]_N]_N\ _N[_N[towel]_N\ _N[rack]_N]_N]_N$ (Selkirk 1982:111)
(g) $_A[_N[head]_N\ _N[_A[strong]_A\ -ness]_N]_N$ (Selkirk 1982:111)
(h) $[[theater]_N [go]_V er]_N$ (Kiparsky 1982:23)

The Category Retention Constraint, it should be noted, does not constitute a special case of some more general constraint such as the Endocentricity Constraint (45) and other functionally related constraints formulated in terms of some notion of percolation. The Category Retention Constraint expresses an identity claim about the relation between a base word to which a WFR applies and a corresponding constituent of the complex word formed by the application of the rule. The Endocentricity Constraint, by contrast, expresses an identity claim about the relation between a particular constituent of a complex word and the word as a whole.

There is no general a priori consideration that I am aware of that leads us to expect a difference in category status between base words and the corresponding constituents of morphologically complex words. To find appropriate empirical justification for the Category Retention Constraint, however, is not a straightforward matter. In this connection consider again the category status of ent_1 and ent_2 as constituents of the reduplication ent-ent. The Category Retention Constraint predicts that ent_1 and ent_2 will, like the base ent, belong to the category Noun. This claim is difficult to test empirically because <u>ent</u>$_1$ and <u>ent</u>$_2$, as is predicted by the Morphological Island Constraint (5), are not accessible to inflectional, derivational and syntactic processes.

This is to say that it is not possible to determine whether <u>ent</u>$_1$ and <u>ent</u>$_2$ are treated as nouns by the relevant inflectional, derivational and syntactic rules. The question, then, is whether there are phonological and/or semantic interpretation rules whose formulation requires <u>ent</u>$_1$ and <u>ent</u>$_2$ to be assigned the status of nouns. Since this study does not deal primarily with the specification of the phonological properties of Afrikaans reduplications, I am unable to say how rules of Afrikaans phonology bear on it. In §3.17 below I will take up this question with reference to the interpretation rule to be proposed for such reduplications.

The view that the lexical category of the base of a reduplication is carried over to both of its constituents requires Afrikaans reduplications to be bracketed as in (120)(c) and not as in (120)(a) or (b).

(120) (a) $[\alpha_i\ \alpha_i]$
(b) $[\ [\alpha_i]\ \alpha_i]$[39]
(c) $[\ [\alpha_i]\ [\alpha_i]\ ]$

Only (120)(c) provides the brackets that are needed for assigning a lexical category label to both constituents of a reduplication.[40]

Applied in conjunction with the Open Category Constraint (30), the Endocentricity Constraint (45), and the Category Retention Constraint (118), the formation rule (2) will generate reduplications with the following morphological representations:

(121) (a) $[\ [\alpha_i]_N\ [\alpha_i]_N]_N$ (e.g., <u>bal-bal</u>, <u>ente-ente</u>, <u>tien-tien</u>)
(b) $[\ [\alpha_i]_V\ [\alpha_i]_V]_V$ (e.g., <u>voel-voel</u>, <u>brul-brul</u>)
(c) $[\ [\alpha_i]_{Adj}\ [\alpha_i]_{Adj}]_{Adj}$ (e.g., <u>saam-saam</u>, <u>vaak-vaak</u>)

2.8 Number of constituents

All the Afrikaans reduplications considered so far have two main constituents. That is, all these reduplications are formed by copying the base once only. And reduplications in which the base has been copied more than once are, in fact, ill-formed in Afrikaans.

(122) (a) Die kinders drink bottels-bottels limonade.
the children drink bottles bottles lemonade
(b) *Die kinders drink bottels-bottels-bottels
the children drink bottles bottles bottles
limonade.
lemonade
(c) *Die kinders drink bottels-bottels-bottels-bottels
the children drink bottles bottles bottles bottles
limonade.
lemonade

(123) (a) Hulle speel weer bal - bal.
they play again ball ball
(b) *Hulle speel weer bal - bal - bal.
they play again ball ball ball
(c) *Hulle speel weer bal - bal - bal - bal.
they play again ball ball ball ball

(124) (a) Die dokter voel-voel aan die swelsel.
the doctor feel feel on the swelling
(b) *Die dokter voel-voel-voel aan die swelsel.
the doctor feel feel feel on the swelling
(c) *Die dokter voel-voel-voel-voel aan die swelsel.
the doctor feel feel feel feel on the swelling

(125) (a) Hulle eet dik - dik snye brood.
they eat thick thick slices bread
(b) *Hulle eet dik - dik - dik snye brood.
they eat thick thick thick slices bread
(c) *Hulle eet dik - dik - dik - dik snye brood.[41]
they eat thick thick thick thick slices bread

The formation rule (2) does not, however, stipulate the fact that the base (i.e., α) is to be iterated once only. And, indeed, the rule need not state this fact as a language-specific constraint. For this fact is a consequence of a language-independent condition, formulated tentatively by Lieber (1981:173) as the "Multiple Application Constraint" on word formation processes:

(126) No word formation process, e.g., insertion of a given morpheme into a lexical tree, or string-dependent rule, can apply iteratively to its own output.

Whereas Lieber's notion of "insertion of a given morpheme into a lexical tree" includes compounding and affixation, her notion of "string-dependent rule" provides for processes such as reduplication and umlaut. She invokes the Multiple Application Constraint to account for the ill-formedness of Tagalog reduplications (e.g., *ʔipapagbibilih) formed by the double application of reduplication rules, and also for the ill-formedness of complex words formed by the iteration of affixes in, for example, English (e.g., *blueishishish, *unununhappy), German (e.g., *Mädchenchenchen, *Vögleinleinlein), and Spanish (e.g., *pequenitititito, *muchachotototote).

Lieber's formulation of the Multiple Application Constraint is "tentative" in various respects. First, as she notes herself (1981:173), this formulation "... does no more than identify a class of phenomena which seem to share the same property. Within a truly explanatory theory of word formation, it ought to follow from some general property of the theory that multiple applications of word formation processes are unacceptable."

A possibility not considered by Lieber is that this constraint may represent one of the consequences of some version of the semantic constraint formulated as (97) above. Recall that this constraint states that an affix cannot be added to a base that already carries features associated with the affix.

Second, as has often been noted, there are many languages in which compounding rules may apply to their own output. Selkirk (1982:15), for example, has recently restated this observation for English by saying that "compounding is in principle recursive". Thus the rule N → N N, applying recursively to its own output, generates the following:

(127) (a) bath room
(b) bath room towel
(c) bath room towel rack
(d) bath room towel rack designer
(e) bath room towel rack designer training

It is not clear whether the Multiple Application Constraint allows for the recursion evidenced in (127)(b)-(e). It is possible that Lieber would not consider these compounds to be counterexamples to the Multiple Application Constraint. She could contend that all that the constraint was intended to rule out was the repeated addition to a compound ("insertion", in her terminology) of one of the same form. Whether this more restricted interpretation of the constraint would be compatible with compounds such as (128)(b) - cited by Roeper and Siegel (1978:204) - is doubtful, however.

(128) (a) coffee maker
(b) coffee maker maker

In (128)(b), obviously, one and the same form, namely maker, has been iterated.[42]

Applied to a formation rule such as (2), Lieber's Multiple Application Constraint (126) is ambiguous. On one reading it prohibits the iterative addition of more than one copy of the original base of a reduplication. This is the sense in which the constraint has been invoked above to account for the ill-formedness of the Afrikaans reduplications (122)(b) and (c), (123)(b) and (c), (124)(b) and (c), and (125)(b) and (c).

On the other reading, the Multiple Application Constraint disallows the iterative copying of reduplications as wholes. If the constraint were applied to the Afrikaans formation rule (2) on this reading, the underscored reduplications in the (b) sentences below would be expected to be ill-formed.

(129) (a) Die kinders drink bottels-bottels limonade. [= (122)(a)]
(b) Die kinders drink [bottels-bottels]-[bottels-bottels] limonade.

(130) (a) Hulle speel weer bal-bal. [= (123)(a)]
(b) Hulle speel weer [bal-bal]-[bal-bal].

(131) (a) Die dokter voel-voel aan die swelsel. [= (124)(a)]
(b) Die dokter [voel-voel]-[voel-voel] aan die swelsel.

(132) (a) Hulle eet dik-dik snye brood. [= (125)(a)]
(b) Hulle eet [dik-dik]-[dik-dik] snye brood.

The prediction is correct: as reduplications, i.e., as morphologically complex words, the forms underscored in the (b) sentences above are in fact ill-formed. Note that these reduplications differ in structure from the corresponding (e) forms in (122)-(125). This point may be illustrated with respect to the reduplications in (122)(e) and (129)(b), the former having the structure (133), the latter the structure (134).

(133) [[bottels] [bottels]] [bottels]] [bottels]]
[(122)(c)]

(134) [[[bottels] [bottels]] [[bottels] [bottels]]]
[(129)(b)]

Given then the ambiguity in question, the Multiple Application Constraint correctly rules out both the multiple copying manifested by (133) and that displayed by (134).

In sum: restrictions on the multiple application of the formation rule (2) do not represent a peculiarity of Afrikaans grammar. Rather, they instantiate a constraint on WFRs that is specific neither to one particular language nor to one particular type of WFR - a conclusion that further advances the demystification of Afrikaans reduplication. This conclusion is independent of the ultimate formulation of the Multiple Application Constraint or that of the more fundamental principle under which this constraint might be subsumed.[43]

2.9 Nature of morphological operation

Let us consider next the consequences of the assumption that the formation rule (2) performs a copying operation. Two obvious consequences may be formulated in negative terms, as (135) and (136).

(135) Afrikaans reduplication does not represent a process of compounding.

(136) Afrikaans reduplication does not represent a process of affixation.

It will be shown below that these consequences are correct in an interesting way, their correctness not being a matter of mere definition.

2.9.1 Compounding

Consider the idea that Afrikaans reduplication is a process of compounding, contrary to what (135) asserts. There are two *a priori* reasons for entertaining this idea as a working hypothesis. The first such reason is historical: the more detailed conventional studies have generally assumed that this is the case. Kempen (1969:136, 184, 341, etc.), for example, explicitly refers to Afrikaans reduplications as "compounds" (= "komposita") and includes both reduplications and "nonreduplicated" compounds in the same comprehensive taxonomy of Afrikaans compounds. He does not, however, present any justification for this step.

The second *a priori* reason why Afrikaans reduplications may be viewed as putative compounds is of a systematic linguistic nature. Corresponding to each lexically distinct type of reduplication, Afrikaans has a type of "nonreduplicated" compound. Compare the compounds in (137)(b) with the reduplications in (a), for example.

(137) (a)	(i)	$[N - N]_N$	(b)	(i)	$[N + N]_N$
		bal - bal			tennis + bal
		ball ball			tennis ball
		ent - ent			teer + ent
		stretch stretch			asphalt stretch
		bottels-bottels			bier + bottels
		bottles bottles			beer bottles
	(ii)	$[V - V]_V$		(ii)	$[V + V]_V$
		skop-skop			skep + skop
		kick kick			scoop kick
					"drop(-kick)"
		loop-loop			storm + loop
		walk walk			storm walk
					"charge"

	stap-stap		draf + stap
	walk walk		trot walk
			"go at a slow trot"
(iii)	$[Adj\text{-}Adj]_{Adj}$	(iii)	$[Adj+Adj]_{Adj}$
	arm - arm		arm + salig
	poor poor		poor blessed
			"poor/pitiful"
	dom - dom		dom + astrant
	stupid stupid		stupid cheeky
			"impudent"
	blou-blou		donker + blou
	blue blue		dark blue
(iv)	$[Adv\text{-}Adv]_{Adv}$	(iv)	$[Adv+Adv]_{Adv}$
	ongeërg-ongeërg		gemaak + ongeërg
	casual casual		affectedly casual
	rooi-rooi		dik + rooi[44]
	red red		thick red
	skelm-skelm		gemeen + skelm
	sly sly		mean sly

To generate the (b) compounds of (139), rules - or functionally equivalent devices - such as the following are required.

(138) (i) N → N N (for (137)(b)(i))

(ii) V → V V (for (137)(b)(ii))

(iii) Adj → Adj Adj (for (137)(b)(iii))

(iv) Adv → Adv Adv (for (137)(b)(iv))

These compounding rules appear, moreover, also to generate the morphological structures of the respective lexically distinct types of reduplication listed in (137)(a)(i)-(iv). And, provided that the same lexical item is inserted under both preterminal nodes of each binary morphological structure, these reduplications seem to be generated automatically by the compounding rules (138) and the rule(s) of (morpho-) lexical insertion. It would be attractive from a systematic point of view, then, to assume that Afrikaans reduplications are in fact compounds. The grammar under this assumption would not need to incorporate a distinct formation rule such as (2).

Given the differences between the properties of reduplications and those of "nonreduplicated" compounds, however, the claim that Afrikaans reduplication is a compounding process cannot be upheld.

First, whereas compounds in Afrikaans may have a hierarchical structure formed by means of recursion, reduplications have a "flat" binary structure that does not allow recursion. This is why the compounds (139)(a)(ii) and (iii) are well-formed but the reduplications (139)(b)(ii) and (iii) are ill-formed.

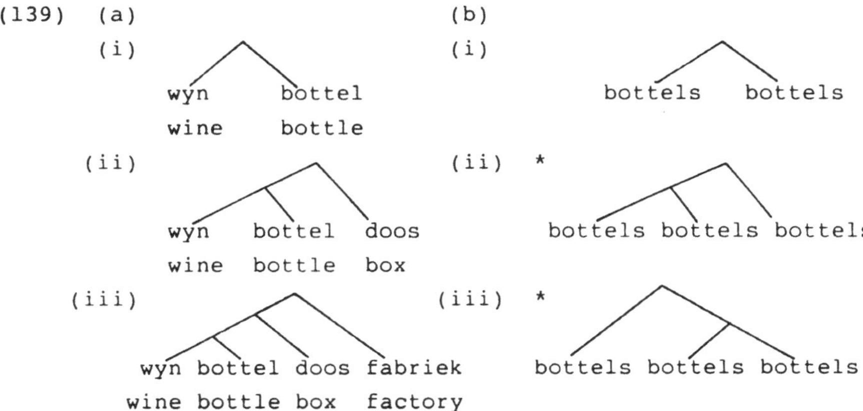

Second, there are (morpho)phonological and semantic differences between Afrikaans compounds and reduplications which are incompatible with the assumption that compounding and reduplication instantiate the same morphological process in Afrikaans. To begin with: the phonological form of the left-hand constituent of certain compounds displays a type of allomorphy not exhibited by the corresponding constituent of lexically related reduplications.[45] For example, as left-hand constituent of compounds of the type N + N, the lexical item *heks* ([hɛks]) has the form [hɛksə], *skip* ([skəp]) the form [skep], *kind* ([kənt]) the form [kəndər], and *dokter* ([dɔktər]) the form [dɔktərs].

(140) (a)	hekse + dans	hekse + besem	hekse + tand
	witch's dance	witch's broom	witch's tooth

(b)	skeeps + reis boat trip	skeeps + dokter ship's doctor	skeeps + ramp ship disaster
(c)	kinder + hand child's hand	kinder + kuns child art	kinder + roof child stealing
(d)	dokters + besoek doctor visit	dokters + geld doctor money	dokters + mes doctor's knife

As the left-hand constituent of reduplications, however, heks, skip, kind, and dokter do not exhibit the allomorphy illustrated in (140):

(141) Die kinders speel heks - heks / skip-skip / kind-
the children play witch witch / ship ship / child
kind / dokter-dokter.
child / doctor doctor
"The children are playing 'witches'/'ships'/'children'/ 'doctors'."

The left-hand constituent of Afrikaans reduplications, in fact, never exhibits this kind of allomorphy. The difference in allomorphy between Afrikaans compounds and reduplications indicates that the right-hand constituent of a compound "dominates" the left-hand one in some way, whereas the right-hand constituent of a reduplication does not "dominate" the left-hand one.[46] If compounding and reduplication created formal structures of essentially the same sort, one would not expect this kind of difference to exist.

Turning to the stress pattern of Afrikaans reduplications, we observe that it differs systematically from that of lexically related compounds of the type considered above. This point may be illustrated with reference to noun-based reduplications and N + N compounds. The vast majority of N + N nominal compounds are forestressed (´ `).[47]

(142)	dókters + gèld doctor's money	tól + tỳd top time
	hékse + bèsem witch's broom	wínkel + mèisie shop girl

All Afrikaans reduplications, however, have level or double stress (´´), including those based on the nouns that appear as left-hand constituents in the compounds of (142).[48]

(143) Die kinders speel dókter-dókter/héks-héks/ tól-tól/wínkel-wínkel.

Consider next the semantic composition of Afrikaans reduplications. This differs fundamentally from that of lexically related compounds of the type considered above. Informally, these compounds have a semantic composition in which the meaning of the left-hand constituent may be said to modify that of the right-hand one. To put it in referential terms: the left-hand constituent delimits or individuates a specific subset of the set of objects denoted by the right-hand one.

Thus, in the case of the compound doktersmes, dokters restricts the objects denoted by mes (= "knife") to a specific subset, namely that used by a doctor. The semantic composition of a reduplication such as dokter-dokter cannot, however, be characterized in similar terms. That is, the semantic composition of reduplications is not such that the meaning of a given constituent may be said to "modify" that of the other constituent in the sense illustrated above.[49] In traditional terms, the right-hand constituent of the compounds under consideration thus constitutes the "semantic head".[50] The right-hand constituent of Afrikaans reduplications, of course, cannot be characterized in these terms.

The formal difference between Afrikaans compounds and reduplications considered above would not be consonant with the assumption that reduplication is a compounding process in Afrikaans. Moreover, it is not clear how the grammar of Afrikaans would be able on this assumption to capture the phonological and semantic differences between these reduplications and compounds without the aid of ad hoc devices. The latter differences may be accounted for, however, if the semantic and phonetic interpretation of Afrikaans reduplications and compounds are based on different formal structures.

2.9.2 Affixation

This brings us to (136), the claim that Afrikaans reduplication does not represent a process of affixation. There is no analysis of Afrikaans reduplication on which this process is construed as (a form of) affixation, as far as I know.

Recently, however, Marantz (1982:436), working within an autosegmental framework, has claimed that the reduplication rules of Tagalog and a number of other languages "... are normal affixation processes". On his view, "... the one unique feature of reduplication, the feature which leads us to group together diverse morphological processes under the title reduplication, is the resemblance of the added material to the stem being reduplicated".[51]

Marantz proposes his analysis for a phenomenon that is distinct from Afrikaans reduplication, however. He (1982:437-38) draws a distinction between processes that copy "constituents of morphemes" and processes that copy "entire morphemes or words", restricting the term "reduplication" to the former and calling the latter "constituent copying". Afrikaans reduplication clearly instantiates Marantz's "constituent copying". It does not interact with phonological processes in such a way as to create the kinds of problems for the solution of which Marantz has to assign reduplication in Tagalog and other languages the status of affixation rules. That is, there is no explanatory advantage in viewing Afrikaans reduplication as an affixation process. On the contrary, adopting such a view of Afrikaans reduplication would have unwelcome consequences within the framework of the present study. One of these would be the creation of a wholly unconstrained notion of "affix". In terms of this notion, any kind of unit that may be copied and "affixed", would, by definition, have the status of "affix", including morphologically noncomplex words, derived and inflected words, and compounds (cf. §2.3 above). But these kinds of "affixes" would exhibit none of the distinctive properties of the morphological units that are considered affixes outside the framework of an affixation analysis of reduplication. In sum: the claim that Afrikaans reduplication does not represent a process of affixation is justified by its consequences.

2.9.3 Copying

The claim that Afrikaans reduplication is a copying process likewise has a set of clear positive consequences. These are, in essence, that the copy created by the formation rule (2) will have all and only the properties of the base that has been copied by the rule.[52] It is predicted, in other words, that the left-hand and right-hand constituents of Afrikaans reduplications will have exactly the same properties.

Preceding paragraphs have already presented evidence that bears out this prediction. §2.3 has made it clear that the two constituents exhibit the same (internal) morphological structure (cf. (18), (20)-(23)). §2.4 has made it clear that the two constituents manifest the same morphological category type (cf. (28)-(29)). §§2.4 and 2.7 have made it clear that the two constituents belong to the same lexical category (cf. (31)-(35)). §2.9.1, moreover, noted that the two constituents do not differ in ways that require one of them to be assigned the status of head and the other that of nonhead. In addition, §2.9.1 illustrated that the two constituents have the same allomorphic shape (cf. (141)) and the same stress level (cf. (143)). And, as was also noted in §2.9.1, the two constituents do not differ semantically in a way that requires one of them to be viewed as a modifying and the other as a modified constituent. Finally, the semantic composition of Afrikaans reduplications, as we will see in Chapter 3 below, is such as to preclude any claim that one of their constituents has a unit of meaning not shared by the other.

In short, the identity displayed by the two constituents of reduplications in regard to their form, their phonological shape, and their meaning bears out the hypothesis that Afrikaans reduplication represents a copying process. This identity, moreover, is consonant neither with the assumption that Afrikaans reduplication is a compounding process nor with the view that it represents an affixation process.

2.10 Retrospect

The following have been the main findings of the preceding analysis of the formation of Afrikaans reduplications:

1. Afrikaans has only one rule for the formation of reduplications, namely Copy α or $\alpha_i \rightarrow [\alpha_i\ \alpha_i]$, which is a rule of word formation.
2. This formation rule need not stipulate
   (a) the (morphological) category type of the bases to which it applies,
   (b) the category type of the constituents of the reduplications which it forms,
   (c) the lexical category of the bases to which it applies,
   (d) the lexical category of the reduplications which it forms,
   (e) the lexical category of the constituents of the reduplications which it forms,
   (f) the number of times that it may apply to its own output.
3. The properties (a)-(f) of Afrikaans reduplication(s) are specified by general lexicalist constraints on word formation rules - constraints which are all rule-type independent and, with one possible exception, language-independent as well.
4. The category type of the bases to which the formation rule applies is specified by a general constraint which states that all regular word formation processes are word-based.
5. The category type of the constituents of the reduplications generated by the formation rule is specified by a general constraint which, by implication, says that the constituents of morphologically complex words cannot themselves have the status of words.
6. The lexical category of the bases to which the formation rule applies is specified by a constraint which says that Afrikaans WFRs of all major types apply to words of all open categories and to words of open categories alone.

7. The lexical category of the reduplications generated by the formation rule is specified by a general constraint which says that the category of a derived word is always non-distinct from the category of its head (and, consequently, that Afrikaans has no exocentric reduplications).
8. The number of times that the formation rule may apply to its own output is specified by a general constraint which says that no word formation process can apply iteratively to its own output.
9. The copying operation performed by the formation rule is distinct from both compounding and affixation.
10. The formation rule both feeds, and is fed by, other Afrikaans WFRs.

These findings provide a clear illustration of what may be gained by doing morphological analysis in the Galilean style. Afrikaans reduplication, conventionally depicted as a morphological process of bewildering formal complexity, has on our Galilean analysis been found to be a quite simple means of word formation. Its seeming complexity may be reduced to a single simple formation rule which - interacting with general conditions of a language-independent sort - unifies what initially appeared to be an array of diverging formal properties. And the "facts" which were taken by conventional studies as indicative of the apparent formal complexity have been found to represent fictions.

2.11 Consequences

Let us consider briefly some of the consequences of the findings listed above.

2.11.1 Language-specific consequences

At a language-specific level, the findings clearly imply that conventional analyses have wrongly depicted Afrikaans reduplication as being a highly complex morphological process. First, these studies either implicitly or explicitly make the incorrect claim that Afrikaans has a large number of distinct rules for the formation of reduplications. Explicated systematically, this claim entails that Afrikaans has a separate formation rule for each distinct lexical category to which the bases may belong and, in addition, that each of these rules has a separate sub-rule for each distinct lexical category to which reduplications as wholes may belong. As has been argued in the preceding sections, however, Afrikaans has only one rule for the formation of reduplications.

Second, when explicated systematically, conventional studies are seen to make the incorrect claim that Afrikaans reduplication creates a considerable measure of exocentricity in the lexicon of the language. In the preceding sections, by contrast, it has been argued that no exocentricity is created by this process.

Third, conventional studies have incorrectly made out Afrikaans reduplication to be a process that is quite complex from a general-linguistic point of view. Because of an inability to distinguish between the features of this process that manifest language-independent and rule-type independent principles and the features that are language-specific and rule-type specific, these studies have in fact presented all the features of the process as idiosyncratic of Afrikaans. The preceding sections have shown that, viewed from the perspective of putative language-independent constraints on word formation, Afrikaans reduplication exhibits very little idiosyncrasy: on the whole it manifests features of word formation that are language-independent and rule-type independent.

2.11.2 General-linguistic consequences

This brings us to the consequences that the conclusions of §2.10 have at a language-independent level, or, more precisely, at a "non-language-specific" level. The analysis presented in the preceding sections claims that the formation of Afrikaans reduplications is subject to certain general-linguistic constraints on WFRs. This analysis furnishes a modest measure of justification for considering the general purport of these constraints to be neither rule-type specific nor language-specific. Since the scope of the analysis has been restricted to one type of WFR in one language only, it cannot yield much information about the precise formulation that these constraints should ultimately receive. This, however, is not to say that the general-linguistic consequences of the analysis are without significance. So let us consider the constraints in question separately.

To start with the Word-base Constraint (16): in order to meet the condition of descriptive adequacy, quite a number of recent studies have proposed morphological analyses that violate the former constraint.[53] The status of this constraint, consequently, has become rather unclear. The present analysis indicates at least that a constraint with the general purport of (16) is neither language-specific nor rule-type specific, since (16) was motivated initially with reference neither to Afrikaans nor to reduplication rules. What such a constraint would ultimately entail in regard to scope and content, of course, cannot be established on the basis of an analysis of one particular type of WFR, reduplication, in one specific language, Afrikaans.

The present analysis bears in a parallel manner on three other constraints, namely the Morphological Island Constraint (16) (that has a variant known as the "Lexical Integrity Hypothesis"), the Endocentricity Constraint (45), and the Multiple Application Constraint (126). It provides evidence that there are language-independent and rule-type independent constraints with the general purport of (16), (45) and (126) or more general constraints of which the latter three constitute special cases.

As regards the Open Category Constraint (39), this study by its very nature cannot provide grounds for assigning it the status of a language-independent constraint. In the discussion above, however, it has become clear that the notion pertinent to this constraint is that of "open category" and not that of "major category" (as used in lexicalist syntax). It is significant, too, that the notion of "open category" has in fact been widely used in nonlexicalist analyses of lexical mechanisms in languages other than Afrikaans.[54]

Concerning the Category Retention Constraint (118): the analysis of the formal properties of reduplication provides no evidence for this constraint. And, as has been noted above, it is difficult to reconcile this constraint with the Morphological Island Constraint, for which there is cross-linguistic evidence. This, of course, does not exclude the possibility that the constraint may be motivated with reference to phonological and/or semantic properties of Afrikaans reduplications. To the possible semantic relevance of the constraint, I will return in §3.17.2 below.

Let us consider, in conclusion, a general-linguistic consequence of the reduplication analysis that bears on the organization of the lexicon rather than on constraints on WFRs. Specifically, consider the conclusion that the formation rule for Afrikaans reduplications both feeds other Afrikaans WFRs and is fed by them. It was argued above - in §§2.2 and 2.3 - that the other WFRs referred to in this conclusion include inflectional, derivational, and compounding rules. A consequence of this conclusion is that any general model of lexicalist morphology will be inadequate if it structures the lexicon in such a way, or orders the various types of morphological rules in such a way, as to make it impossible for the above-mentioned feeding relations to be captured. For example, a model that makes use of level-ordering without allowing the output of higher levels to serve as input to lower levels won't be able to account for the relationship of mutual feeding that holds between the formation rule for Afrikaans reduplications and other Afrikaans WFRs.

3 Semantic interpretation

3.1 Outline

As was noted in Chapter 1 above, Afrikaans reduplications are held in conventional analyses to be highly complex from the semantic point of view. That is, they are held to express a large set of often diverse "meanings" even though they are all built on a single formal pattern. Accordingly the process of Afrikaans reduplication is likewise taken to be a phenomenon of great semantic complexity. The present analysis, however, will claim that this semantic complexity is apparent rather than real and that all Afrikaans reduplications undergo one and the same semantic interpretation rule, namely (1).

(1) Interpret $[\alpha_i \ \alpha_i]$ as [A INCREASED]
(where A represents the sense or meaning of α and INCREASED represents an abstract semantic unit)

With the specifics of the interpretation rule (1) I will deal below. All that needs to be noted at this point is that rule (1), formulated in the spirit of the Galilean style, is strongly unifying in that it applies to all reduplications. And it is quite simple as well. The central question to be answered is how so simple a rule is able to account for the diversity in and specificity of the meanings conventionally attributed to Afrikaans reduplications. It is to this question that the present chapter will address itself.

The general thesis that will be argued is that both the diversity of the meanings associated with Afrikaans reduplications and the specificity of these meanings are a function of the interaction between the interpretation rule (1) and semantic and/or general conceptual devices that are independent of it. Once the latter devices have been identified and their contribution to the (diversity and specificity of the) meanings of reduplications has been pinpointed, the single interpretation rule (1) will be seen to give an adequate characterization of the semantic content expressed by reduplication in Afrikaans. In accordance with the Galilean style, the diversity and specificity of these meanings will thus be shown to pose no epistemological threat to the unifying rule of interpretation (1). The natural point of departure for the discussion is the diversity of the meanings attributed in conventional studies to Afrikaans reduplications and the process by which Afrikaans reduplications are formed.

3.2 Survey of meanings

Conventional analyses have claimed that reduplication is used in Afrikaans for the expression of both referential or descriptive and nonreferential or nondescriptive meanings. In A-M below, I list the referential meanings to begin with. The core of the list of these meanings comes from the work of Kempen (1969). To the list I have added a number of meanings of the sort found in Kempen's study but, for apparently accidental reasons, not mentioned explicitly by him, Scholtz (1963) or other Afrikaans grammarians. For each meaning I present an abstract characterization (underscored), a concise paraphrase (in inverted commas), and a number of sentences containing reduplications that express it. In the paraphrases "R" will be used to represent the referent to which a base (α) refers via its meaning (A).

A *considerable number*: "many Rs"

(2) (a) Die kinders drink bottels-bottels limonade.
the children drink bottles bottles lemonade
"The children drink bottles and bottles of lemonade."

(b) Bakke-bakke veldblomme versier die tafels.
bowls bowls wild flowers decorate the tables
"The tables are decorated with wild flowers by the bowlful."

B *limited number*: "some Rs"

(3) (a) Die pad was ent - ent sleg.
the road was stretch stretch bad
"The road was bad in some (scattered) stretches."

(b) Jan vergeet sy vrees ruk - ruk.
John forget his fear time time
"Occasionally John forgets about his fear for a while."

C *distribution*: "scattered Rs"

(4) (a) Die skape wei troppe-troppe op die vlakte.
the sheep graze flocks flocks on the plain
"The sheep are grazing on the plain in several scattered flocks."

(b) Die gras het kol - kol verdroog.
the grass has patch patch withered
"The grass has withered in (some) scattered patches."

D *serial ordering*: "the one R after the other"/"R by R"

(5) (a) Hy krap die verf laag - laag af.
he scrapes the paint layer layer off
"He scrapes the paint off in one layer after another."

(b) Die studente skryf die eksamen stuk - stuk.
the students write the exam piece piece
"The students write the exam in instalments."

E *collectivity/grouping*: "in more than one group of R"/
"in one group of R after the other"

(6) (a) Hy dra tien-tien boeke die trap op.
he carry ten ten books the stairs up
"He carries the books up the stairs in one ten-book batch after another."

(b) Susan sluk die pille drie - drie in.
Susan swallow the pills three three in
"Susan swallows the pills in sets of three."

F *iteration*: "to R more than once/repeatedly"

(7) (a) Hy lek - lek oor sy droë lippe.
he lick lick over his dry lips
"He licks and relicks his dry lips."

(b) Sy kop knik-knik van vermoeienis.
his head nod nod of weariness
"His head repeatedly nods with weariness."

G *continuation*: "to R continuously/for some time"

(8) (a) Die donder rammel-rammel in die verte.
the thunder rumble rumble in the distance
"A continual rumble of thunder may be heard."

(b) Die bedelaar drentel-drentel doelloos in
the beggar saunter saunter aimlessly in
die park rond.
the park about
"The beggar has been sauntering aimlessly in
the park for some time."

H *attenuation*: "to R (more than once) tentatively/
hesitantly/non-intensely"

(9) (a) Die dokter vat - vat aan die swelsel.
the doctor touch touch on the swelling
"The doctor tentatively feels the swelling a
couple of times."

(b) Hy skop-skop teen die deur.
he kick kick against the door
"He gives the door a few exploratory kicks."

I *simultaneity*: "while R-ing simultaneously/at the same time"

(10) (a) Die leeu loop brul-brul weg.
the lion walk roar roar away
"Roaring, the lion walks away."

(b) Die tuinier sny sing-sing die grasperk.
the gardener mow sing sing the lawn
"The gardener sings as he mows the lawn."

J *alternation/interruption*: "with R alternating with R'/
interrupting R'" (where R'
is the referent of the main verb)

(11) (a) Hy loop staan-staan die gang af.
he walk stand stand the corridor down
"He walks haltingly down the corridor."

(b) Sy doen die werk rus - rus.
she do the work rest rest
"She does the work stopping frequently to rest."

K *manner*: "R-ing to do R'/as a means of doing R'"

(12) (a) Die man loop skuifel-skuifel oor die straat.
the man walk shuffle shuffle across the street.
"The man crosses the street with a shuffling gait."

(b) Sy drink slurp-slurp haar tee.
she drink sip sip her tea
"She drinks her tea by sipping it."

L *intensity*: "very R"

(13) (a) Hulle eet dik - dik snye brood.
they eat thick thick slices bread
"They eat thumping thick slices of bread."

(b) Sy het amper - amper haar been gebreek.
she has nearly nearly her leg broken
"She very nearly broke her leg."

M *emphasis*: "emphatically/specifically/definitely/just R"

(14) (a) Die ongeluk het hier-hier gebeur.
the accident has here here happened
"The accident happened right here/on this very spot."

(b) Hulle doen die werk saam - saam.
they do the work together together
"They do the work very much as a team effort."

Before looking at the non-referential meanings attributed to reduplication in Afrikaans, we have to consider a number of general points in connection with the referential meanings listed above.

First, as regards the origin of these meanings, the majority are due to Kempen (1969) and Scholtz (1963). Their work, however, makes only implicit provision for the distinction between "considerable number" (A) and "limited number" (B), that between "serial ordering" (D) and "collectivity/grouping" (E), and that between "simultaneity" (I), "alternation/interruption" (J) and "manner" (K). No explicit provision, moreover, is made for "attenuation" (H).

Second, the meanings listed above are taken in conventional studies to be "atomic" in some sense, i.e. not decomposable into "more primitive" meanings. The glosses given above have been constructed so as to illustrate the individual "atomic" meanings. On conventional analyses, however, a single reduplication may express more than one "atomic" meaning or may be ambiguous between various "atomic" meanings. Kempen (1969: 346), for example, characterizes the meaning of verb reduplications such as lek-lek (= "lick lick") in (7)(a) and rammel-rammel (= "rumble rumble") in (8)(a) as "durative and iterative", where "durative" represents our "continuation" (G). He (1969:341) states that brul-brul (= "roar roar") in (10)(a), staan-staan (= "stand stand") in (11)(a) and skuifel-skuifel (= "shuffle shuffle") in (12)(a) "indicate manner with respect to a verb, and are generally durative and/or iterative too". Consider as a final example the reduplication twee-twee (= "two two") in the following sentence.

(15) Die motors het twee-twee daar geparkeer gestaan.
the cars have two two there parked stood
"The cars had been parked there in pairs."

On Scholtz's (1963:156) analysis the meaning expressed by reduplicated "numerals" such as twee-twee is "partly iterative, partly distributive". To this composite meaning Kempen (1969: 289) adds a third element when he states that "Perhaps (a) group value or (a) grouping value should therefore in addition be added to (Scholtz's) iterative/distributive (values)." On Scholtz's and Kempen's analyses twee-twee in (15) would express the "atomic" meanings "distribution" (C), "iteration" (F) and "collectivity/grouping" (E). Notice, incidentally, how many hedges and other obscure expressions occur in the quoted claims by Scholtz and Kempen. It is often difficult to determine what is claimed by conventional studies about the meaning of specific reduplications.

Third, with reference to the (composite) meaning assigned by Kempen and Scholtz to the form twee-twee, it is possible to indicate a general problem that the linguist encounters when attempting to establish the meaning of Afrikaans reduplications. Kempen's and Scholtz's claims about the meaning of twee-twee express intuitive judgments for which no justification is furnished. When one attempts to check these judgments against those of linguistically unsophisticated native speakers, it soon becomes clear that such intuitive semantic judgments are highly variable. Different native speakers make different intuitive judgments about the meaning of the same reduplication. In addition, the judgments of linguistically skilled native speakers about the meaning of the same reduplication often differ in subtle ways. Evidence to settle such differences is on the whole not easy to come by, as will be illustrated below with respect to reduplications that are claimed to denote games played by children. In short, to assign a specific meaning to a given reduplication is often to do no more than express an intuitive judgment.

Fourth, quite a number of the informal descriptive notions used in conventional analyses are less than sufficiently clear. This is true of conventional analyses not only of Afrikaans reduplication but of reduplication in other languages as well. Consider as a case in point the distinction drawn between the notions of "intensity" (L) and "emphasis" (M).[1] Conventional studies fail to make clear in what nonintuitive sense "emphasis" differs from "intensity", or where, say, "intensity" stops and "emphasis" begins.

Moreover, given that this distinction does have an empirical basis, such studies fail to make clear whether it should be captured in referential (semantic) or non-referential (pragmatic) terms.

The notion of "manner", as used in K above, further illustrates the insufficient clarity of the conventional descriptive notions. This notion of "manner", in fact, is really just a device for indicating a general respect in which the meaning of <u>skuifel-skuifel</u> in (18) differs from that of <u>sing-sing</u> ("simultaneity") in (16) and that of <u>staan-staan</u> ("alternation/interruption") in (17).

(16) 'n Man loop <u>sing-sing</u> oor die straat.
a man walk sing sing across the street
"A man crosses the street, singing as he goes."

(17) 'n Man loop <u>staan-staan</u> oor die straat.
a man walk stand stand across the street
"A man crosses the street, pausing from time to time."

(18) 'n Man loop skuifel-skuifel oor die straat.
a man walk shuffle shuffle across the street
"A man shuffles across to the other side of the street."

Kempen (1969:341), in fact, uses a notion of "manner" that even includes "simultaneity" and "alternation/interruption" too.[2]

Let us now consider the nonreferential meanings or functions attributed to Afrikaans reduplications. A first such meaning has conventionally been characterized as a "stylistic function of a general sort". Though it is claimed that Afrikaans reduplications may be used in all styles and registers, it has been noted that such forms are characteristic of less formal styles and registers. The nature of these styles and registers has conventionally been indicated by means of expressions such as "intimate",[3] "colloquial",[4] "jovial",[5] "dramatic",[6] "affective" and "vivid".[7] A speaker of Afrikaans may use reduplications, therefore, to show that he would like to enter into or establish a less formal relationship with the other participant(s) in the speech situation.

It has been claimed that certain reduplications do not differ in regard to referential meaning from their bases at all. Noun reduplications that denote games played by children constitute a case in point.

(19) Hulle speel weer bal - bal.
they play again ball ball
"They are playing their ball game again."

(20) Hulle speel elke dag tol-tol.
they play every day top top
"They play (at) tops every day."

(21) Knoop - knoop is 'n gewilde speletjie.
button button is a popular game
"The game played with buttons is popular."

On Kempen's (1969:236) judgment, for example, the reduplication tol-tol (= "top top") in (20) does not "say anything more" than the nonreduplicated tol in (22).

(22) Hulle speel elke dag tol.
they play every day top
"They play (at) tops every day."

If judgments such as these were correct - whether they are is a question to which I will return in §3.14 below - reduplications of this type would have only the general nonreferential function considered above.

A second and more specific nonreferential function is restricted to the type of reduplication occurring in the following sentences.

(23) Die meisie staan vaak - vaak op.
the girl get sleepy sleepy up
"The girl, still slow with sleep, gets up."

(24) Die meisie laat skaam-skaam haar kop hang.
the girl let shy shy her head hang
"Shyly, the girl lets her head hang."

(25) Die meisie sit die borde traag - traag weg.
the girl put the plates reluctantly reluctantly away
"Reluctantly, the girl puts the plates away."

On Kempen's (1969:138-139) analysis the underscored reduplications are "intensifying and emphatic", thus expressing a specific referential meaning. Linguistically sophisticated speakers, however, do not judge the difference in meaning between these reduplications and the corresponding nonreduplicated forms underscored in (26)-(28) to be primarily one of intensity.

(26) Die meisie staan vaak op.
the girl get sleepy up
"The girl gets up sleepy."

(27) Die meisie laat skaam haar kop hang.
the girl let shy her head hang
"Shyly, the girl lets her head hang."

(28) Die meisie sit die borde traag weg.
the girl put the plates reluctantly away
"Reluctantly, the girl puts the plates away."

On the judgment of such speakers, a person who gets up "vaak-vaak" is not sleepier than one who gets up "vaak". And they have analogous judgments on the difference between "skaam-skaam" and "skaam" as well as that between "traag-traag" and "traag".[8]

Further probing of the semantic judgments of such speakers has revealed that they "feel" the above-mentioned reduplications to differ primarily in the following way from their non-reduplicated bases: reduplications such as vaak-vaak, skaam-skaam, and traag-traag convey a sense of empathy not expressed by the nonreduplicated forms. That is, by using such reduplications these speakers appear to indicate that they are able to enter into the feelings, motives, etc. of the agents of the sentences, that they can readily understand or appreciate these feelings, motives, etc. The native speakers under consideration point out that the latter sense is more aptly labelled "empathy" than "sympathy", the latter term being "too strong". Expressing "empathy", then, is the second and more specific nonreferential function of reduplication in Afrikaans.[9]

3.3 The interpretation rule for reduplications

The interpretation rule (1) assigns to an Afrikaans reduplication $[\alpha_i \alpha_i]$ the semantic reading [A INCREASED], where [A] represents the meaning or sense of the unreduplicated base form α, and [INCREASED] an abstract semantic unit. The qualification "abstract" indicates that, as a semantic unit, [INCREASED] is not to be identified with the linguistic expression increased. To distinguish a meaning or semantic unit from a linguistic expression, I will represent the former by means of capitals and enclose it in square brackets. Following Jackendoff (1983:36), both a meaning or sense and an abstract semantic unit will be considered a unit of information that represents an aspect of conceptual structure. On this view, the information conveyed by a linguistic expression is not about the real world but about the projected world, i.e., about the world as experienced by the human mind.[10] The entities referred to by linguistic expressions, on this view, are to be found in the projected world, not the real world. These entities include, in Jackendoff's (1983:50) terminology, things, places, directions, actions, events, manners, amounts, etc.[11] Against this background, the interpretation rule (1) may be understood as saying that by reduplicating a base form, the information is conveyed that the entity (or entities) in the projected world referred to by the base form is taken to be increased in some dimension.

The question is how the single interpretation rule (1) could account for the diversity and specificity of the referential meanings listed in A-M in §3.2 above. But note the underlying assumption being made here about the assignment of all the various meanings to the respective reduplications with which they are associated. It is assumed that the assignment of meanings is performed by rule (1) operating in isolation. Such a "splendid isolation" assumption is simply wrong, however, since it reflects a failure to distinguish between the total information content associated with/expressed by individual reduplications and the semantic content that may be expressed by the formal process of reduplication. This failure, of course, puts the assumption at odds with the fact that the semantic content expressed by reduplication contributes only one of the components of the total information content associated with individual reduplications. The problems with the "splendid isolation" assumption may ultimately be reduced to a conception of "meaning" that fails to allow for the fact that the total information content associated with a linguistic form is decomposable into various components belonging to different classes.

Against this background, the paragraphs below will present a reanalysis of the so-called referential meanings A-H and L-M associated with Afrikaans reduplications. This reanalysis will proceed from the assumption that each of these meanings constitutes an amalgam of units of information that are not all attributable to the same source. The interpretation rule (1), in fact, contributes only one unit of information to the amalgam. It will be shown that, given an adequate characterization of the contributions made by other devices to the total information content of reduplications, and of the way in which these devices interact with the interpretation rule (1), there are no grounds either for having more than one semantic interpretation rule for Afrikaans reduplications, or for complicating the rule (1).

Within the framework of the individual reanalyses, the devices involved in the composition of the total information content of Afrikaans reduplications will be represented informally only. That is, in presenting these reanalyses, I will attempt to steer clear of technical controversies such as the one about whether certain units of information should be represented formally by means of semantic markers or by some other kind of device. And in presenting the individual reanalyses, I will not consider the question of whether a given unit of information - or the rule specifying it - constitutes part of linguistic meaning or, alternatively, represents an aspect of extra-grammatical belief, knowledge of the world or some other nonlinguistic conceptual system. I will use expressions such as "meaning", "semantic reading/unit", and "(unit of) information content" informally as synonyms. The neutral expression "conceptualization rules" will be used to denote an important subset of the devices that interact with the interpretation rule (1). General theoretical issues, including questions about the linguistic and methodological status of the conceptualization rules, will be discussed in §3.15 below. Note also that in the reanalyses that will follow, I am not implicitly claiming either that the various decompositions of the conventional meanings cannot be carried further, or that completely exhaustive decomposition of the meaning of (complex) lexical items is in principle possible. The proposed decompositions are presented with the sole purpose of identifying those semantic components that are relevant to the argument that there is only one interpretation rule for Afrikaans reduplication, namely (1). A final word of caution: the reanalyses of the conventional meanings should not be interpreted as informal semantic derivations. In presenting these reanalyses I do not advocate any position on how semantic derivations should be generated.

Note that the meanings I (= "simultaneity"), J (= "alternation"/"interruption"), and K (= "manner") will not be subjected to reanalysis below. As was argued in §2.6.4 above, the forms with which these meanings are associated do not have the status of reduplications. These forms are morphologically complex words derived by means of zero affixation. The interpretation rule (1) need obviously not account for the semantic interpretation of nonreduplications. Nor of course does this rule have to account for the nonreferential meanings associated with Afrikaans reduplications. As is clear from such work as, for example, Dressler's (1968:82) and Samarin's (1978), the nature of the relationship between referential and nonreferential meanings deserves an analysis the scope of which would take us beyond the confines of the present study. We can now move on to a reanalysis of the referential meanings listed as A-H, L and M above.

3.4 Considerable number ("many Rs")

The total information content associated with reduplications such as bottels-bottels (= "bottles bottles") in (2)(a) and bakke-bakke (= "bowls bowls") in (2)(b) may be analyzed in the following way:

(a) The lexical base (bottels, bakke) contributes two units of meaning that account for the value of A. The first is the unit [BOTTLE]/[BOWL] associated with the non-affixal constituent (bottel, bak) as specified in the dictionary of the language, the second the plurality meaning [MORE THAN ONE] associated with the affix (-s). Jointly, these two units form the composite reading [BOTTLE/BOWL, MORE THAN ONE].

(b) The interpretation rule (1) contributes the unit of meaning [INCREASED]. The semantic contribution of the base and that of the interpretation rule jointly form the composite reading [BOTTLE/BOWL, MORE THAN ONE, INCREASED].

(c) A conceptualization rule specifies that the unit of meaning [INCREASED] must be interpreted numerically because the A with which it has to be amalgamated includes the semantic unit [COUNTABLE THING].[12] For later reference this rule may be formulated as follows:

(29) Conceptualize [INCREASED] as [INCREASED IN NUMBER] if it occurs in conjunction with the semantic specification [COUNTABLE THING].

The unit of information contributed by the conceptualization rule (29) to the total information content of Afrikaans reduplications, clearly, is independent of the unit of information contributed by the interpretation rule (1). It follows, then, that the information expressed by rule (29) need not and, indeed, should not be accounted for by the interpretation rule itself.

(d) A second conceptualization rule applies to the reading [BOTTLE/BOWL, MORE THAN ONE, INCREASED IN NUMBER] to amalgamate the units of meaning [INCREASED IN NUMBER] and [MORE THAN ONE]. This rule may be formulated as follows:

(30) Conceptualize [INCREASED IN NUMBER] and [MORE THAN ONE] jointly as [CONSIDERABLE NUMBER] or [MANY].

Applied to [BOTTLE/BOWL, MORE THAN ONE, INCREASED IN NUMBER] this rule yields the more complex unit of content [BOTTLE/BOWL, CONSIDERABLE NUMBER/MANY]. Note that the semantic contribution of the conceptualization rule (30) need not be accounted for by the interpretation rule (1).

3.5 Limited number ("some Rs")

The composition of the total information content associated with reduplications such as <u>ent-ent</u> (= "stretch stretch") in (3)(a) and <u>ruk-ruk</u> (= "time time") in (3)(b) may be described as follows:

(a) The lexical base (<u>ent</u>, <u>ruk</u>) contributes the unit of meaning, [STRETCH]/[TIME], that represents the value of A. This unit of meaning is specified in the dictionary of the language.

(b) The interpretation rule (1) contributes the unit of meaning [INCREASED], giving the composite reading [STRETCH/TIME, INCREASED].

(c) The conceptualization rule (29) specifies, as in the case of <u>bottels</u> and <u>bakke</u>, that [INCREASED], when in conjunction with an A such as [STRETCH] or [TIME], must be interpreted numerically as [INCREASED IN NUMBER] since [STRETCH] and [TIME] include the semantic unit [COUNTABLE THING] in their internal make-up.

(d) However, ent and ruk, unlike bottels and bakke, do not incorporate a plural affix and their meaning lacks the unit [MORE THAN ONE]. Alternatively, the meaning of these bases may be analyzed as incorporating the semantic unit [(NOT MORE THAN) ONE]. As a result the conceptualization rule (30) does not apply in the case of ent-ent and ruk-ruk and the composite reading [STRETCH/TIME, CONSIDERABLE NUMBER/MANY] is not derived. A different conceptualization rule, which may be a subcase of (30), applies to [STRETCH/TIME, (NOT MORE THAN) ONE, INCREASED IN NUMBER].

(31) Conceptualize [INCREASED IN NUMBER] and [(NOT MORE THAN) ONE] jointly as [LIMITED NUMBER/SOME].

The difference in total information content between "many Rs" and "some Rs" thus reduces to the semantic contribution of a plural affix that does not form part of the bases of reduplications such as ent-ent and ruk-ruk. And so the difference in total information content between reduplications such as bottels-bottels and reduplications such as ent-ent need not be accounted for by the interpretation rule (1).

3.6 Distribution ("scattered Rs")

The total information content associated with reduplications such as troppe-troppe (= "flocks flocks") in (4)(a) and kol-kol (= "patch patch") in (4)(b) is more complex than the total information content of reduplications such as bottels-bottels (= "bottles bottles") and ent-ent (= "stretch stretch"). The former content, in fact, represents an extension of the latter.

(a) As expressed by troppe-troppe, the composite content "scattered Rs" includes "many Rs" as a component and, as expressed by kol-kol, it includes "some Rs" as a component. The composition of "many Rs" and "some Rs" has been described above.

(b) A conceptualization rule specifies that the semantic units [MANY] and [SOME] must be interpreted distributively because the meanings with which these have to be amalgamated include the semantic unit [BOUNDED MEASURE]. This rule may be formulated as follows:

(32) Conceptualize [MANY Rs] and [SOME Rs] as respectively [MANY Rs, DISTRIBUTED] and [SOME Rs, DISTRIBUTED] if the former semantic units occur in conjunction with the semantic unit [BOUNDED MEASURE].

As noted by Jackendoff (1983:246, n. 9), things may be bounded or unbounded at a conceptual level. Bounded things have some kind of boundary - e.g., a spatial boundary in the case of physical objects - but unbounded things are referred to in such a way that boundaries are not part of the picture conveyed.[13] If the bounded things are measure units of a specific magnitude - as in the case of a bottle, a bowl, a stretch, a patch, etc. - they have to be distributed or scattered in some dimension. If measure units of a specific magnitude were not scattered in some dimension, they could not constitute more than one unit of the magnitude in question, but would rather collectively constitute a single unit of a larger magnitude (denoted, perhaps, by a different lexical item). The conceptualization rule (32) thus, expresses the following idea:

(32') For there to be more than one distinct unit of quantity, volume, length, etc. of a specific magnitude, the units have to be non-adjacent, i.e., scattered or distributed, in some dimension.

Concretely, if we took the base noun <u>kol</u> to denote a patch, a number of patches would simply constitute a larger single spatial unit, unless they were conceptualized as being distributed, i.e., as separated by intervening "nonpatches". To multiply bounded things that constitute measure units of a specific magnitude, thus, entails conceptualizing them as being distributed or scattered. The conceptualization rule (32) expresses this generalization by applying to composite readings such as [FLOCK, MANY] and [PATCH, SOME] and deriving from these the more composite readings [FLOCK, MANY, DISTRIBUTED] and [PATCH,

SOME, DISTRIBUTED] respectively. Notice, incidentally, that the traditional term "distributive plural" may be aptly applied to reduplications such as troppe-troppe and kol-kol.

The conclusion to be drawn, therefore, is that [DISTRIBUTED] as a component of the total information content of reduplications such as troppe-troppe, kol-kol, etc. does not represent a unit of information contributed by the morphological process of reduplication and should not be specified by an interpretation rule such as (1). [DISTRIBUTED] as a unit of content is derived by means of an independent conceptualization rule such as (32). In §3.16 below I will explore the possibility that [DISTRIBUTED] rather than [INCREASED] is the fundamental unit of meaning expressed by rule (1).

3.7 Serial ordering ("the one R after the other")

The total information content associated with reduplications such as laag-laag (= "layer layer") in (5)(a) and stuk-stuk (= "piece piece") in (5)(b) is composed in essentially the same way as that of the distributive plurals troppe-troppe (= "flocks flocks"), kol-kol (= "patch patch"), etc. From the point of view of their total content, reduplications such as laag-laag, stuk-stuk, etc. are distributive plurals too, a point that may be illustrated with reference to laag-laag.

(a) The total information content of laag-laag, like that of kol-kol, incorporates the semantic unit [LIMITED NUMBER]/[SOME] that is derived in the way described in §3.5 above with reference to ent-ent, etc.

(b) The content of laag-laag, again like that of kol-kol, incorporates in addition the component [DISTRIBUTED]. The difference in total content between kol-kol and laag-laag may be reduced to a difference between the dimensions in which the units/entities denoted by the respective base forms are distributed. In the case of kol-kol the dimension is spatial; in the case of laag-laag, etc. the dimension is non-spatial - temporal or "logical". To say that entities are "serially ordered" is, in fact, to say that they are distributed in time or in "logical" space. The lexical meaning of its base and the linguistic and non-linguistic context in which a given reduplication occurs provide clues about the nature of the dimension in which the distribution of scattering must be construed, a point that will be taken up again in §3.15.3 below.

[ORDERED SERIALLY], therefore, is not a unit of content to be specified by a semantic interpretation rule such as (1). Consequently, the difference in total content between reduplications such as *laag-laag* and reduplications such as *kol-kol* should not be accounted for by this rule either.

3.8 Collectivity ("in more than one group of R")

The total information content attributed to reduplications such as *tien-tien* (= "ten ten") in (6)(a) and *drie-drie* (= "three three") in (6)(b) is also an amalgam of various units of meaning.

(a) The lexical base (*tien*, *drie*) contributes two units of meaning to fix the semantic content of α. This point may be illustrated with reference to *tien* (= "ten") and *drie* (= "three"). On the one hand *tien* and *drie* contribute a unit of meaning in virtue of which they are different cardinals. This unit of meaning is [TEN] in the case of *tien* and [THREE] in the case of *drie*. On the other hand, *tien*, *drie* and the other cardinals have a shared unit of meaning which they contribute to the content of α. Recall that §§2.5 and 2.6.5 above argued that cardinals such as *tien* and *drie* have the formal properties of group nouns. "Numeral" group nouns share a unit of meaning with "nonnumeral" group nouns such as *klomp* (= "lot"), *groep* (= "group"), *horde* (= "horde"), etc. This unit of meaning may be represented as [GROUP] or [COLLECTION]. As group nouns *tien* and *drie*, therefore, have the composite meanings [TEN, GROUP] and [THREE, GROUP] respectively.[14]

(b) The interpretation rule (1) contributes the semantic unit [INCREASED] to the total information content of the reduplications under consideration, yielding [TEN, GROUP, INCREASED] and [THREE, GROUP, INCREASED].

(c) The conceptualization rule (29) specifies that, since the meaning with which [INCREASED] has to be amalgamated includes the semantic specification [COUNTABLE THING] - groups are countable entities - [INCREASED] has to be conceptualized numerically. That is, [INCREASED] and, for example, [TEN, GROUP] must jointly be conceptualized as [TEN, GROUP, INCREASED IN NUMBER].

(d) The latter composite reading, in fact, also includes the unit of meaning [(NOT MORE THAN) ONE] - the base form groep does not incorporate a plural affix. Consequently, the conceptualization rule (31) comes into play and the composite reading [TEN, GROUP, LIMITED NUMBER/SOME] is formed.

(e) To the latter reading the conceptualization rule (32) adds the semantic unit [DISTRIBUTED], yielding [TEN, GROUP, LIMITED NUMBER/SOME, DISTRIBUTED]. An analogous reading is derived for drie-drie. Unless the groups of, for example, ten were distributed, there would not be more than one group of ten but simply one larger group of, say, twenty, thirty, etc. In regard to content, therefore, tien-tien and drie-drie are in fact distributive plurals like bottels-bottels and kol-kol. The distribution may be in a spatial dimension as in Hulle staan drie-drie in die saal (= "They stand about in the hall in scattered groups of three") or in a temporal dimension as in Hulle verlaat die saal drie-drie (= "They leave the hall in one group of three after another"). Clues about the nature of this dimension are provided by the linguistic context, central to which are the respective lexical meanings of the verb and of the constituents structurally related to the verb.

The general point is that the interpretation rule (1) need not contribute more than the semantic component [INCREASED] to the total content of these reduplications, the other components being furnished from independent sources.

3.9 Iteration ("to R repeatedly")

We consider next the total information content associated with verb reduplications such as lek-lek (= "lick lick") in (7)(a) and knik-knik (= "nod nod") in (7)(b).

(a) The lexical base (lek, knik) contributes two units of meaning to the total semantic content of α. The first unit distinguishes the meaning of, for example, lek [LICK] from that of knik [NOD], and other nonsynonymous lexical items. The second is a unit shared by the meaning of lek, and the meaning of knik. This unit of meaning may be characterized as [TEMPORAL ACT/EVENT].[15]

(b) The interpretation rule (1) contributes the unit of meaning [INCREASED] to the total information content of the reduplications under consideration.

(c) A conceptualization rule specifies how [INCREASED] has to be conceptualized in conjunction with the meanings of lek and knik respectively. Since the meaning of neither lek nor knik includes the semantic unit [COUNTABLE THING], rule (29) is inapplicable and [INCREASED] will not be conceptualized numerically as [INCREASED IN NUMBER]. Since the meaning of both lek and knik incorporates the semantic unit [TEMPORAL ACT/EVENT], the following conceptualization rule applies to [LICK, TEMPORAL ACT/EVENT, INCREASED] and [NOD, TEMPORAL ACT/EVENT, INCREASED].

(33) Conceptualize [INCREASED] as [INCREASED IN TIME] if it occurs in conjunction with the semantic unit [TEMPORAL ACT/EVENT].

Given this rule, the composite readings [LICK, TEMPORAL ACT/EVENT, INCREASED IN TIME] and [NOD, TEMPORAL ACT/EVENT, INCREASED IN TIME] may be formed.

(d) In these two composite readings, however, the unit [INCREASED IN TIME] is only partially amalgamated with the semantic units [LICK] and [NOD]. The reason for this is that licking and nodding represent a particular kind of temporal act or event: in the terminology of Jackendoff (1983:246) they are temporally bounded events or acts. This feature of the projected referent of the verbs lek and knik may be represented in their meaning by the semantic unit [BOUNDED] which constitutes a unit of so-called aspectual meaning.[16] To amalgamate the semantic unit [INCREASED IN TIME] with [BOUNDED] a conceptualization rule with the content of (34) is required:

(34) Conceptualize the unit of content [INCREASED IN TIME] as [ITERATED] if it occurs in combination with the unit of aspectual meaning [BOUNDED].

Clearly, a bounded event can occur for an increased time only if it is conceptualized as being repeated more than once. Applied to the readings specified in (a) above, the conceptualization rule (34) forms [LICK, TEMPORAL ACT/EVENT, ITERATED] and [NOD, TEMPORAL ACT/EVENT, ITERATED].

As a unit of meaning, then, [ITERATED] need not be specified directly by an interpretation rule such as (1). It is a derived unit, established through the interaction of this rule with the conceptualization rules (33) and (34). Note that the extension of the parameter of boundedness from things to acts/events is crucial to this analysis.[17]

3.10 Continuation ("to R continuously")

The total information content associated with verb reduplications such as rammel-rammel (= "rumble rumble") in (8)(a) and drentel-drentel (= "saunter saunter") in (8)(b) is parallel, in composition, to that of iterative reduplications such as lek-lek (= "lick lick") and knik-knik (= "nod nod"). The difference between iteration and continuation reduces to a difference in aspectual meaning between lek-lek and knik-knik on the one hand and rammel-rammel and drentel-drentel on the other hand. The base verbs of the former type have the unit of aspectual meaning [BOUNDED], the base verbs of the latter the unit of aspectual meaning that Jackendoff (1983:246) calls [UNBOUNDED]. This implies that the unit of aspectual meaning [UNBOUNDED] forms part of the composite readings [RUMBLE, TEMPORAL EVENT, UNBOUNDED, INCREASED IN TIME] and [SAUNTER, TEMPORAL EVENT, UNBOUNDED, INCREASED IN TIME]. To these composite readings the conceptualization rule (35) applies.

(35) Conceptualize the unit of content [INCREASED IN TIME] as [CONTINUED] if it occurs in combination with the unit of meaning [UNBOUNDED].

What this rule says, in essence, is that by increasing an unbounded temporal event one gets a single extended event of the same sort. Applied to the composite readings under consideration, rule (35) gives [RUMBLE, TEMPORAL EVENT, CONTINUED] and [SAUNTER, TEMPORAL EVENT, CONTINUED].

The distinction between iteration and continuation, therefore, reflects an aspectual difference between the base verbs of reduplications. This distinction is acted on by different conceptualization rules or different subcases of the same, more general, conceptualization rule. In sum: the distinction between iteration and continuation clearly need not be accounted for directly by the interpretation rule (1).[18]

3.11 Attenuation ("to R more than once non-intensely")

The total information content associated with reduplications such as vat-vat (= "touch touch") in (9)(a) and skop-skop (= "kick kick") in (9)(b) incorporates what appears to be a mysterious component. This component, which has conventionally been characterized as "tentatively/hesitantly/non-intensely", will be represented below by the abstract specification [ATTENUATED]. The question is how this unit can be a component of a composite content to which the interpretation rule (1) contributes the semantic unit [INCREASED]. As part of the total information content of verb-based reduplications one would expect the latter unit to be conceptualized on an intensity scale as "more intensely" rather than "less intensely", "tentatively", etc. Closer analysis shows, however, that there is in fact nothing mysterious about the way in which the unit [ATTENUATED] is derived as a component of the information content of reduplications such as vat-vat and skop-skop.

(a) The bases (vat, skop) of such reduplications are verbs that have the unit of aspectual meaning [BOUNDED]. The reduplications, consequently, are assigned an iterative reading in the way described in (d) of §3.9 above.

(b) The unit of content [ATTENUATED] represents another derived component of the total information content of verb-based reduplications such as vat-vat, skop-skop, etc. Let us consider the following sentences to get a better grasp of the nature of this unit of meaning.

(36) (a) Hy skop-skop teen die deur. [= (9)(b)]
he kick kick against the door
"He tentatively kicks the door a couple of times."

(b) Hy sluit-sluit die deur.
he lock lock the door
"He tentatively locks the door a couple of times."

The total information content of skop-skop in (36)(a) includes both the components [ITERATED] (expressed by "a couple of times" in the paraphrase) and [ATTENUATED] (expressed by "tentatively" in the paraphrase). Native speakers of Afrikaans intuitively judge this sentence as "making sense", etc. If sentence (36)(b) is interpreted in a parallel way, however, speakers judge this sentence to be "nonsensical", "illogical", etc.

This difference in acceptability between the two sentences may be explained indirectly with reference to the nature of the events or acts denoted by skop and sluit respectively. Note that the event/act denoted by sluit has a certain conclusiveness or finality. The event/act denoted by skop, by contrast, lacks this feature: it is inconclusive or non-final. Obviously, it is impossible to repeat an event/act that has this property of finality in a relatively short time-span. And this is why sentence (36)(b) is "nonsensical" to speakers of Afrikaans. To put it differently, the finality of the event/act of locking something precludes the possibility of its occurring repeatedly within the same short time-span, without the intervention of another act/event, specifically an "unlocking" event/act. In the case of skop, by contrast, the event/act lacks this finality. Consequently, it may be repeated within a relatively short time-span. For this reason native speakers have no problem in "making sense" of sentence (36)(a).

The essence of the semantic difference between reduplications such as sluit-sluit and reduplications such as skop-skop may, therefore, be captured by the following generalization.

(37) If an event/act has the property of finality, it cannot occur/be performed more than once in a relatively short time-span.

Evidently, events/acts that have the property of finality cannot occur/be performed less intensely. That is, such events/acts cannot be attenuated. The repeatability of an act/event, thus, indicates its attenuability. The repetition of an event may therefore be interpreted as an indication of its attenuation on a scale of intensity. Notice that what we have here is not logical entailment but rather the weaker relation of indication.

The question, of course, is how the difference between the events/acts denoted by sluit and those denoted by skop may be expressed by a conceptualization rule operating on the semantic units composing the meanings [LOCK] and [KICK]. Finding an answer to this question is a matter of determining whether the difference can be accounted for in aspectual terms. Note that verbs such as sluit denote events/acts that have been called "achievements" by Vendler (1967:103). On his view, an achievement - e.g., to arrive at a destination, to win a race, to reach the top of a hill, to forget or remember something - is an event or act that occurs at a single moment and cannot be extended in time or, I think one should add, be repeated in a relatively short time-span.[19] As noted by, for example, Platzack (1979:71), achievements constitute a special type of bounded event/act characterizable by the semantic unit [PUNCTUAL EVENT/ACT]. Events/acts characterized by the kind of finality under consideration, accordingly, are punctual events/acts too. But punctuality is an aspectual parameter, which means that the correspondence between punctuality and finality makes it possible to capture the essence of the generalization (37) by a conceptualization rule formulated in terms of aspectual notions.

(38) Conceptualize [ITERATED] in conjunction with the unit of aspectual meaning [NONPUNCTUAL] as [ITERATED AND ATTENUATED].

The conceptualization rule (38) says that the repetition of a nonpunctual event/act indicates its attenuation. [ATTENUATED], therefore, is a derived unit of meaning associated with reduplications whose verb bases have the aspectual meanings

[BOUNDED] and [NONPUNCTUAL]. On the basis of (39), it is predicted that punctual verbs, i.e. verbs denoting achievements, cannot be reduplicated in Afrikaans. This prediction is borne out by the semantic oddity of sentences such as the following:

(39) (a) *Hulle <u>arriveer-arriveer</u> môre.
they arrive arrive tomorrow
"*They tentatively arrive a couple of times tomorrow."

(b) *Tenzing <u>bereik-bereik</u> die kruin van Everest.
Tenzing reach reach the summit of Everest
"*Tenzing tentatively reaches the summit of Everest a couple of times."

(c) *Zola <u>wen-wen</u> die wedloop.
Zola win win the race
"*Zola tentatively wins the race a couple of times."

(d) *Hy <u>onthou-onthou</u> die voorval.
he recall recall the incident
"*He tentatively recalls the incident a couple of times."

In sum: since the semantic unit [ATTENUATED] is derived by means of a conceptualization rule, it need not, and should not, be specified by the semantic interpretation rule (1).

3.12 Intensity ("very R")

The composition of the total information content associated with reduplications such as <u>dik-dik</u> (= "thick thick") in (13)(a) and <u>amper-amper</u> (= "nearly nearly") in (13)(b) may be described as follows:

(a) The lexical bases <u>dik</u> and <u>amper</u> contribute the respective units of meaning [THICK] and [NEARLY] to the total information content.

(b) The interpretation rule (1) contributes the semantic unit [INCREASED].

(c) A conceptualization rule specifies that the meaning [INCREASED] must receive an intensity interpretation because the meaning of the base with which it has to be amalgamated includes the semantic unit [VARIABLE/GRADABLE QUALITY].[20] This rule, which belongs to the same family as (29) and (33), may for further reference be formulated as follows:

(40) Conceptualize [INCREASED] as [INCREASED IN INTENSITY]/ [INTENSIFIED] if it occurs in conjunction with the semantic unit [VARIABLE/GRADABLE QUALITY].

As parameters of qualities, variability and gradability are in an intuitive sense parallel to boundedness as a parameter of things and acts/events. The specification "VARIABLE/GRADABLE" may therefore be replaced by "UNBOUNDED"in (40).

Be that as it may, [INTENSIFIED], as a component of the information content of reduplications, need not be specified directly by the interpretation rule (1): it results from the interaction between the semantic contribution of this rule, a component of the lexical meaning of the bases of reduplications, and the conceptualization rule (40).

3.13 Emphasis ("emphatically R")

The total information content associated with reduplications such as hier-hier (= "here here") in (14)(a) and saam-saam (= "together together") in (14)(b) resembles that of dik-dik (= "thick thick") and amper-amper (= "nearly nearly") in regard to internal composition. The difference between "intensity" and "emphasis" reduces to a difference in lexical meaning between hier-hier and saam-saam on the one hand and dik-dik and amper-amper on the other hand. It was noted above that the lexical meaning of the bases of reduplications such as dik-dik and amper-amper includes the semantic unit [VARIABLE/GRADABLE QUALITY]. The lexical meaning of the bases of forms such as hier-hier and saam-saam, by contrast, incorporates the semantic unit [NONVARIABLE/NONGRADABLE ATTRIBUTE]. When in conjunction with the latter unit, [INCREASED] cannot receive an intensity interpretation, since intensity presupposes variability. Therefore it must be the conceptualization rule (41), rather than (40), that applies in the case of hier-hier and saam-saam.

(41) Conceptualize [INCREASED] as [INCREASED IN SPECIFICITY]/ [EMPHASIZED] if it occurs in conjunction with the semantic unit [NONVARIABLE/NONGRADABLE ATTRIBUTE].

Given the parallelism between variability/gradability and boundedness observed in §3.12, the specification "BOUNDED" could be substituted for "NONVARIABLE/NONGRADABLE" in (41).

The rule (41) says in effect that [INCREASED], when in conjunction with [NONVARIABLE/NONGRADABLE ATTRIBUTE], may be conceptualized as emphasizing the idea that it is this quality, and not one of the conceivable alternatives, that is pertinent to or characteristic of a given situation. An increase in the attribute of "here-ness" or "being here", for example, has to be thought of as "precisely/specifically/just/right here and definitely not in any other conceivable place". Characterized in these terms, the derived meaning under consideration resembles Dressler's (1968:83) "asseverative" variant of emphasis.

The distinction between "intensity" and "emphasis", therefore, is a function of a difference in lexical meaning between base forms of reduplications such as dik-dik and amper-amper on the one hand and of reduplications such as hier-hier and saam-saam on the other hand. It is, therefore, yet another instance of a distinction that need not and should not be accounted for directly by an interpretation rule such as (1).

3.14 Threats to the analysis

Let us consider briefly a number of apparent limitations of this analysis of the semantics of Afrikaans reduplication. Recall that the device central to this analysis is the interpretation rule (1) of §3.1 by which the semantic unit [INCREASED] is assigned to every reduplication generated by the formation rule (2) of §2.1 as a component of its total information content. There are various reduplications which appear to be counterexamples to the former interpretation rule. Since it would be unwise to summarily give up a rule with the unifying power of (1), I will defend this interpretation rule in the Galilean style against the negative impact of the apparent counterexamples. Specifically, in §§3.14.3 and 3.14.4, I will question the factual status of the more interesting "counter-examples", reanalyzing them in such a way that they cease to pose a threat to the interpretation rule.

3.14.1 Lexicalized meanings

The interpretation rule (1), in conjunction with the other conceptual devices considered in the preceding sections, does not account for the lexicalized meanings of some Afrikaans reduplications. This point may be illustrated with reference to the reduplication kort-kort in the following sentence.

(42) Hy besoek ons kort - kort.
he visit us short short
"He drops in every now and again."

Given the interpretation rule (1) and the other devices that jointly specify the composition of the content of Afrikaans reduplications, kort-kort should mean "for a very short period". Lexicalized meanings, however, do not constitute a special feature of reduplications: the meanings of many Afrikaans compounds and derived words exhibit such unpredictable elements. Unpredictable elements of meaning, moreover, cannot be accounted for by means of semantic interpretation rules of any generality.

So the inability of the interpretation rule (1) to account for lexicalized meanings is no real shortcoming. The point is not that a grammar should not account for lexicalized meanings; only that it is not the task of a theory of (the semantic interpretation of) reduplications to do so.

3.14.2 Nonreferential meanings

The semantic interpretation rule (1), by its very nature, is unable to account for the nonreferential meanings - such as those discussed in §3.2 above - that reduplication may have in Afrikaans. Stylistic, registral and other pragmatic functions do not constitute a feature that is distinctive of reduplication. It is not clear, moreover, that such functions are among the phenomena to be accounted for by a grammatical theory which purports to be a description of grammatical competence or knowledge of grammar, as opposed to communicative competence.[21] If a grammar did have to account for such functions, the devices required for this would in any case be of a general sort, not specific to a theory of (the semantic interpretation of) reduplications. For this reason I refrain from speculating further about the nature of these devices.

3.14.3 Empathy/intensity readings

At first glance, the application of the interpretation rule (1) to reduplications such as those underscored in (43)-(45) may appear to be problematic.

(43) Die meisie staan vaak - vaak op. [= (23)]
the girl get sleepy sleepy up

(44) Die meisie laat skaam-skaam haar kop hang. [= (24)]
the girl let shy shy her head hang

(45) Die meisie sit die borde traag - traag
the girl put the plates reluctantly reluctantly
weg. [= (25)]
away

In §3.2 above, it was noted that for some native speakers the semantic difference between, on the one hand, vaak-vaak (= "sleepy sleepy"), skaam-skaam (= "shy shy"), and traag-traag (= "reluctantly reluctantly") and, on the other hand, the bases vaak, skaam, and traag is one of "empathy" rather than intensity. The interpretation rule (1), however, assigns these reduplications the semantic unit [INCREASED], which is conceptualized as [INCREASED IN INTENSITY]/[INTENSIFIED] in accordance with the conceptualization rule (40). The question, then, is whether the above-mentioned semantic judgment indicates that reduplications such as vaak-vaak, etc. have to be excluded from the scope of the interpretation rule. My initial conclusion (Botha 1984b:32-133) was that such an exclusion had to be effected in a way that was not clear to me. Further investigation, however, has convinced me that the observational basis of this conclusion is unsound.

To begin with, on the judgment of many native speakers, reduplications such as vaak-vaak, skaam-skaam and traag-traag do have an intensity reading: "very sleepy", "very shy", "very reluctant". These native speakers, significantly, are linguistically untrained. The native speakers who initially judged the primary semantic difference between these reduplications and the corresponding nonreduplicated forms in (26)-(28) above to be one of "empathy" rather than intensity were linguistically trained people: translators and professional linguists. And the latter judgments were elicited from them by means of what now appears to me to have been misleading questions: "Do you judge a person who gets up "vaak-vaak" to be sleepier than one who gets up "vaak"?", etc. A negative reply to this question was, erroneously, taken to imply that for these speakers reduplications such as vaak-vaak did not have an intensity reading. The error of interpretation stemmed from my failure to see that nonreduplicated vaak may denote various degrees of sleepiness, from "only just sleepy" to "very sleepy indeed". Thus, a person who gets up "vaak-vaak" (= "very sleepy") need not be more sleepy than one who gets up "vaak" (= "very sleepy").

Suppose that reduplications such as vaak-vaak in fact did not have an intensity reading for the speakers concerned. One would then expect it to be possible for vaak-vaak, etc. to be accompanied by an intensifying modifier such as baie (= "very"). Though nonreduplicated vaak may be accompanied by such a modifier, the speakers in question judge sentences in which such modifiers are used in construction with vaak-vaak, etc. to be "strange", etc.

(46) (a) Die meisie staan baie vaak op.
the girl get very sleepy up

(b) *Die meisie staan baie vaak - vaak op.
the girl get very sleepy sleepy up

The "strangeness" of sentences such as (46)(b) follows from the assumption that vaak-vaak, etc. has an intensity reading for the speakers in question: double intensification would give baie vaak-vaak, etc. the property of semantic redundancy.

There is a second indication that vaak-vaak has an intensity reading for the speakers under consideration: they judge sentences such as (47)(b) to be "bizarre", "strange", etc. too.

(47) (a) Die meisie staan effens vaak op.
the girl get somewhat sleepy up

(b) *Die meisie staan effens vaak - vaak op.
the girl get somewhat sleepy sleepy up

In (47)(a) the modifier effens (= "somewhat") is used to attenuate vaak, which is possible because vaak may denote varying degrees of sleepiness, including sleepiness of a lesser degree. The "bizarreness" etc. of (47)(b) would follow if the speakers in question assigned an intensity reading to vaak-vaak: to both attenuate and intensify something at the same time gives rise to semantic anomaly. In sum: the strangeness of sentences such as (46)(b) and (47)(b) provides evidence for assuming that the native speakers under consideration do provide for an intensity reading for reduplications such as vaak-vaak, skaam-skaam and traag-traag. This is to say that the semantic judgments of these speakers do not provide evidence for excluding such reduplications from the scope of the interpretation rule (1).

How, then, did these native speakers come to assign an "empathy" reading to the reduplications under consideration? Recall that these speakers were professional translators and linguists, i.e. people with above average skill in using and reflecting on their language. My guess is that, having been misled into thinking that reduplications such as vaak-vaak, etc. did not have an intensity reading, these speakers went on to look for some other contribution of reduplication to the meaning of these forms. In the process they discovered the "empathy" reading and were forced (by the misleading nature of my question) to consider it the primary semantic difference between reduplications such as vaak-vaak, skaam-skaam, traag-traag and the nonreduplicated vaak, skaam, traag. This reconstruction does not deny the existence of the "empathy" reading; it merely suggests why the "empathy" reading was incorrectly judged to represent the primary semantic difference between the former and the latter forms. Notice, incidentally, that in the case of certain reduplications of the vaak-vaak type it would be difficult to arrive at an "empathy" reading.

(48) (a) Die meisie sit die borde vuil - vuil weg.
the girl put the plates dirty dirty away

(b) Die meisie dra die jas stukkend-stukkend
the girl wear the coat torn torn
werk toe.
work to

(c) Die smulpaap eet die slakke rou-rou op.
the gourmand eat the snails raw raw up

In the case of these sentences an "empathy" reading would be available only to those native speakers who are able to understand how it "feels" for a plate to be (put away) dirty, a coat to be (worn) torn or a snail to be (eaten) raw.

3.14.4 Game names

We appear to have a problem as regards the application of the interpretation rule (1) to reduplications such as bal-bal (= "ball ball") in (49), tol-tol (= "top top") in (50), and knoop-knoop (= "button button") in (51).

(49) Hulle speel weer bal - bal. [= (19)]
they play again ball ball
"They are playing their ball game again."

(50) Hulle speel elke dag tol-tol. [= (20)]
they play every day top top
"They play (at) tops every day."

(51) Knoop - knoop is 'n gewilde speletjie. [= (21)]
button button is a popular game
"The game played with buttons is popular."

It was noted in §3.2 above that on Kempen's judgment reduplications such as bal-bal, tol-tol, and knoop-knoop - which denote games played by children - have no element of referential meaning that is not also part of the meaning of their unreduplicated bases. If this judgment were correct, these reduplications would, somehow, have to be excluded from the scope of the interpretation rule (1), so as to prevent them from being assigned the meanings "some balls", "some tops", and "some buttons" respectively. I will argue below that the judgment under consideration is not correct and that reduplications such as bal-bal, tol-tol and knoop-knoop should not be excluded from the scope of this interpretation rule.

It is simply not the case that the reduplications in question do not differ in referential meaning from the corresponding unreduplicated forms. Let us consider this claim with reference to tol-tol, a typical "game name" reduplication. Unlike the unreduplicated form tol, the reduplication tol-tol does not denote just any playful activity involving the use of tops. The reduplication rather denotes a quite specific game - one in which two or more players pursue a clearly defined aim in accordance with fixed rules. The aim of the game and the rules governing it may, at a given time, vary from location to location, and at a given location the rules may be changed from time ("season") to time, but the game as such is never identical to mere playful activity involving the use of tops. Some of the properties of the projected referent of tol-tol are reflected in differences between the meaning of the reduplication and that of the nonreduplicated form tol (which does denote mere playful activity involving the use of tops). Native speakers judge (53), for example, to be semantically "strange" as opposed to (52) and (54), which "make perfect sense" to them.

(52) Hulle speel tol-tol. (conventionalized game,
they play top top two or more players)
"They are playing (at) tops."

(53) *Hy speel tol-tol. (conventionalized game,
he play top top one player only)
"*He is playing (at) tops."

(54) Hy speel tol. (nonconventional playful
he play top activity, one player only)
"He is playing with a top."

And, on the judgment of native speakers, the verb speel (= "play") may be replaced in the sentence (55)(a) by gooi (= "throw") without affecting the meaning or acceptability of the sentence. Substituting gooi for speel in sentence (56)(a), however, yields a sentence that is judged to be semantically deviant.

(55) (a) Kom ons speel tol. (nonconventionalized play-
come we play top ful activity)
"Let's play with our tops."
(b) Kom ons gooi tol.
come we throw top
"Let's spin our tops."

(56) (a) Kom ons speel tol-tol. (conventionalized play-
come we play top top ful activity
"Let's play tops."
(b) *Kom ons gooi tol-tol.
come we throw top top
"*Let's spin (at) tops."

The difference in deviance between (55)(b) and (56)(b) ties in with the difference in meaning between tol-tol and tol. From the entries in the Woordeboek van die Afrikaanse Taal for other reduplications of the same type - e.g., knoop-knoop (= "button button"), klip-klip (= "pebble pebble"), etc. - it is clear that these, likewise, differ in referential meaning from the corresponding unreduplicated forms.

The question, of course, is whether the "game name" reduplications share an element of referential meaning that systematically distinguishes them from their unreduplicated correlates. The sentences (52)-(54) provide a clue to the answer: they suggest that whereas the subject-NP of a sentence including a "game name" reduplication must be plural, the subject-NP of a sentence with the corresponding unreduplicated form need not be plural. Phrased in semantic terms, the meaning of a "game name" reduplication, as opposed to that of the corresponding unreduplicated form, obligatorily includes the component [INVOLVING MORE THAN ONE AGENT]. [AGENT] here is not identical to [PERSON]: one and the same person can occupy more than one agent role, playing a game with or against himself. That is, one and the same person may represent more than one player in a given game. "Game name" reduplications, then, differ systematically from the corresponding unreduplicated forms in regard to the number of agents obligatorily required by the relevant games.

There appear to be other differences too, though it is not easy to tell whether these involve completely independent units of meaning. The games denoted by the reduplications under consideration are highly repetitive in nature: the players take turns to perform the same basic actions, moves, chants, etc. over and over. It may therefore be claimed that the "game name" reduplications incorporate the semantic components [ITERATED (ACTIONS)]/[SUCCESSIVE (ACTIONS)] and [COMPLEMENTARY (ACTIONS)] too. However, games played by more than one player may by their very nature involve iterated or successive and complementary actions. This is to say that, in the case of "game name" reduplications, the latter semantic units may be nonindependent in the sense that they may be derivable from the unit [INVOLVING MORE THAN ONE AGENT] and the composite semantic whole [GAME].

The semantic unit [INVOLVING MORE THAN ONE AGENT] has a different status. Since games do not by their very nature involve more than one player, this semantic unit is independent from [GAME], the composite semantic whole representing the meaning of game. And since a single player may perform actions that are repetitive or successive and complementary the semantic unit [INVOLVING MORE THAN ONE AGENT] does not reduce to (a conjunction of) the units [ITERATED (ACTIONS)]/[SUCCESSIVE (ACTIONS)] and [COMPLEMENTARY (ACTIONS)]. The semantic difference in agency between reduplications such as bal-bal, tol-tol, and knoop-knoop, on the other hand, thus involves an independent semantic unit.

The question is how the latter semantic unit may be accounted for by an analysis to which the interpretation rule (1) is central. This rule applies normally to the "game name" reduplications under consideration, assigning them the semantic unit [INCREASED]. Recall now that the bases of such reduplications denote some kind of playful activity, as in (57) below.

(57) (a) Sy speel bal.
she play ball
"She is playing with a ball."

(b) Hy speel tol.
he play top
"He is playing with a top."

(c) Hulle speel knoop.
they play button
"They are playing with buttons."

The dictionary entry of all nouns that denote playful activity - whether this activity has become conventionalized or not - has to incorporate the semantic unit [NONCOUNTABLE THING]. This is reflected formally by the fact that sentences in which bal, tol and knoop occur in the plural form are deviant.

(58) (a) *Sy speel balle.
she play ball + PLUR

(b) *Hy speel tolle.
he play top + PLUR

(c) *Hulle speel knope.
they play button + PLUR

It thus appears as if the semantic unit [INCREASED] has to be conceptualized in conjunction with [NONCOUNTABLE THING] in the case of "game name" reduplications. This is impossible within the present analysis as there is no conceptualization rule that could amalgamate these two semantic units into a conceptually well-formed composite unit. Observe, however, that base nouns such as bal, tol and knoop denote a kind of playful activity that presupposes volitional control by an agent. These base nouns, thus, have to incorporate in their meaning the semantic specification [INVOLVING (AT LEAST) ONE AGENT]. Since this specification incorporates the semantic unit [COUNTABLE THING], agents being countable, rule (29) can conceptualize [INCREASED] as [INCREASED IN NUMBER] which may be developed further by rule (31), ultimately giving the conceptually well-formed reading [INVOLVING (AT LEAST) MORE THAN ONE AGENT].

The latter semantic specification, which captures the systematic difference in referential meaning between "game name" reduplications and the corresponding unreduplicated forms, is therefore automatically assigned to these reduplications. Our analysis thus also provides the basis for an explanation of the plurality restriction on subject-NPs illustrated by sentences (52)-(54).

As regards the latter restriction, note that it is an instance of the semantic effect of reduplication showing up formally in a different part of sentences that incorporate "game name" reduplications. This is not a property unique to Afrikaans reduplication. Dressler (1968:66ff.) has compiled evidence about quite a number of genetically unrelated languages which indicates that the semantic effects of reduplication of the verb (stem) show up as distributive plurality in either the subject-NP (so-called "Subjektsdistributivität") or an object-NP (so-called "Objektsdistributivität"). For example, in Quileute kwe.'tsa', meaning "he is hungry", forms the base of the reduplication kwe.'k^{u}tsa which means "various people are hungry", a typical case of "Subjektsdistributivität". And application of reduplication in Aztec to pi-tla ("to pick") gives the reduplication pìpi-tla ("to pick many herbs"), a case of "Objektsdistributivität". Thus, the "transferal" of the semantic effect from the reduplicated form to some other constituent of a sentence incorporating the latter form is an independently attested phenomenon. This "transferal", specifically, is not an artefact of the present analysis of the semantics of Afrikaans reduplication.

The latter analysis thus provides a simple account of the systematic difference in referential meaning between "game name" reduplications on the one hand and the corresponding unreduplicated forms on the other hand. The referential meaning of such a reduplication may, in addition, differ in idiosyncratic ways from that of the corresponding unreduplicated form, reflecting unpredictable aspects of the conventionalization of the game denoted by the reduplication. As explained in §3.14.1 above, such lexicalization does not represent a special feature of reduplications and does not bear negatively on the present analysis.

Let us, in conclusion, consider the meaning of Afrikaans "game name" reduplications from a pragmatic point of view. The games denoted by these reduplications are usually played by children, and the means of expression used by the speech registers of children are known to be simpler and less formal than those used by the speech registers of adult speakers. On the basis of considerations such as these, it could be claimed that "game name" reduplications highlight the pragmatic function of reduplication in Afrikaans. This claim may be construed in more than one way. On a first construal, children would be the category of speakers that most frequently used reduplication productively, specifically for the forming of game names. I suspect that this construal would be confirmed by careful observation. On a second construal, the pragmatic function of "game name" reduplications would be that of marking less formal, "colloquial", etc. speech regardless of the age, social status, etc. of the speaker. This construal would be incorrect: "game name" reduplications may be used non-informally in adult registers too. As a matter of fact, in the absence of simple lexical substitutes it is hard to avoid using "game name" reduplications in Afrikaans.

3.14.5 Number and distribution

Pairs of reduplications such as those of (59) signal a problem for which I don't at present have a satisfactory solution.

(59) (a) (i) Die kinders drink <u>bottels-bottles</u> limonade.
the children drink bottles bottles lemonade
(ii) ?Die kinders drink <u>bottel-bottel</u> limonade.
the children drink bottle bottle lemonade
(b) (i) Sy het <u>boeke-boeke</u> gelees.
she has books books read
(ii) ?Sy het <u>boek-boek</u> gelees.
she has book book read
(c) (i) Hy saag <u>takke - takke</u> af.
he saw branches branches off
(ii) ?Hy saag <u>tak - tak</u> af.
he saw branch branch off

The reduplications of the (i)-sentences may be interpreted as expressing "considerable number". The (ii)-sentences, however, are distinctly odd if the reduplications are interpreted as expressing nothing else but "limited number". Why this is so is unclear to me. The "limited number" reading gets better if the reduplications of the (ii)-sentences are used in sentences in which, in addition to "limited number", they clearly express "distribution" as well. And, correspondingly, sentences in which the reduplications of the (i)-sentences above express "distribution" in addition to "limited number" sound strange.

(59') (a) (i) *Hulle het die vat wyn bottels-bottels
they have the barrel wine bottles bottles
leeg gedrink.
empty drink

(ii) Hulle het die vat wyn bottel-bottel
they have the barrel wine bottle bottle
leeg gedrink.
empty drink

(b) (i) *Sy het die Bybel boeke-boeke gelees.
she has the Bible books books read

(ii) Sy het die Bybel boek-boek gelees.
she has the Bible book book read

(c) (i) *Hy saag die boom takke - takke af.
he saw the tree branches branches off

(ii) Hy saag die boom tak - tak af.
he saw the tree branch branch off

So far, a less than purely speculative explanation of the pattern evidenced by (59) and (59') has evaded me.

3.15 Nature of the proposed rules

We come now to the question of the nature of the interpretation rule (1) and the conceptualization rules (29), (30), (31), (32), (33), (34), (35), (39), (40) and (41). This question may be considered from two angles, namely the (non-) uniqueness of the types to which the proposed rules belong, and the (non)ad hocness of the individual rules.

3.15.1 (Non)uniqueness of the rule types

If the rules under consideration were unique in the sense that they did not resemble devices that have been proposed independently in the literature, their legitimacy could be questioned. Specifically, there would be no real gain in adopting a single semantic interpretation rule on the basis of its simplicity and generality if this rule were of a unique sort or if it could not be used without the support of various conceptualization rules of a unique type. That is, an analysis of the semantics of Afrikaans reduplication that used one simple and general interpretation rule that had to be supported by various unique conceptualization rules would be no better than an analysis that required various less simple and general interpretation rules that did not require the support of unique conceptualization rules.

So, let us consider the question of the nature of the proposed interpretation rule and conceptualization rules against the background of the ongoing debate about Chomsky's so-called skepticism about meaning, a debate in which Chomsky, Katz, and Jackendoff have been the main participants. At issue is the general question of whether it is possible in principle to draw a distinction between what may be informally called "linguistic meaning" and "nonlinguistic meaning". The latter includes so-called "extra-grammatical belief", "knowledge about the world", "pragmatic competence", etc. Obviously, it may be asked whether the rules postulated in our analysis of the semantics of Afrikaans reduplication represent aspects of "linguistic" or "nonlinguistic meaning".

The distinction between "linguistic" and "nonlinguistic meaning" has figured recently in Chomsky's (1980:54, 58) decomposition of the notion "knowledge of a language" into "several interacting but distinct components". A first component represents the so-called "computational" aspects of language taken by Chomsky to include "the rules that form syntactic constructions or phonological or semantic patterns of varied sorts". A second component Chomsky calls a "conceptual system" which involves, among other things, "the system of object-reference", "relations such as 'agent', 'goal', 'instrument', and the like". For Chomsky the conceptual system represents part of some nonlinguistic faculty that provides "common sense understanding of the world in which we live". Chomsky (1980: 225) further elucidates the nature of the conceptual system by giving some examples of the beliefs about the world incorporated in it: "When we identify and name an object, we tacitly assume that it will obey natural laws. It will not suddenly disappear, turn into something else, or behave in some 'unnatural' way; if it does, we might conclude that we have misidentified and misnamed it."

Chomsky (1980:225) contends, however, that "It is no easy matter to determine how our beliefs about the world of objects relate to the assignment of meanings to expressions. Indeed, it has often been argued that no principled distinction can be drawn." He (1980:247) emphasizes the intricacy of this "delimitation" or "parcelling out" problem when he states that "we have already noted how difficult it is - *if indeed it is possible in principle* [my italics, R.P.B.] - to distinguish between semantic properties that are simply language-dependent and others that relate to our beliefs about the natural world".

In subjecting Chomsky's various statements of the "delimitation" problem to critical analysis, Katz (1980:7ff.; 1981: 117ff.) is less skeptical than Chomsky about the possibility of drawing a principled distinction between "linguistic meaning" and what he also calls "extragrammatical belief". Katz's (1981:124) position, in a nutshell, is that this delimitation may be achieved by attempting to construct a theory of semantics whose domain is initially specified as including intuitively "clear cases" of semantic properties and relations:

> As long as, at each point, the semantic system set up for the clear cases decides the unclear ones, and incorrect decisions are eventually revised in subsequent extensions of the semantic system, then automatically the simplest semantic system that ultimately predicts the clear cases of semantic properties and relations will correctly decide the unclear cases and thereby the boundary questions for the domain of semantics.

Katz (1981:119) argues that Chomsky and others have in fact followed this methodological strategy in delimiting the domains of phonology and syntax. He claims that there is a level of autonomous semantic representation. This level provides a description of that aspect of sentence structure responsible for such semantic properties and relations as synonymy, meaninglessness, ambiguity, redundancy, and so on. This level, moreover, determines the application of the laws of logic. Katz thus views meaning and logical form as constituting a single level which represents the literal meaning of sentences. Pragmatic information and encyclopedic knowledge can, on Katz's view, be excluded from meaning/logical form.

Jackendoff (1981) has argued that Katz's defense of autonomous semantics is wanting. The gist of Jackendoff's argument is that there cannot be a single level of semantic representation that is exclusively devoted to expressing literal meaning and that is also the domain over which semantic properties and relations are formally defined. He argues that, if the semantic theory proposed by Katz exists, it either excludes many fundamental phenomena which are normally thought of as semantic or else misses linguistically significant generalizations. Specifically, Jackendoff (1981:431) argues that

> If a theory of 'semantic competence' exists that is autonomous from pragmatic considerations and that is responsible to linguistically significant generalization, we have seen here that it must either include focus and presupposition, or exclude logical inference (§2); it must either include scope of negation and quantifiers, or exclude logical inference and contradiction (§3); and it must either include pronoun-antecedent relations, or exclude contradiction (§4). Moreover, §5 has shown that the proper place to draw the line must be to include the theory of contradiction with the clearly pragmatic cases.

This, Jackendoff (1981:432) finds, does not leave much of autonomous semantics as Katz intended it.

To my knowledge, Katz has not published a rebuttal of Jackendoff's criticisms, the main thrust of which appears to be forceful. Consequently, within the framework of interpretive semantics, in its current state, it is pointless to ask whether the rules postulated by our analysis of the semantics of Afrikaans reduplication represent aspects of "linguistic" or aspects of "nonlinguistic meaning". This, however, is not to say that the nature of these rules is obscure.

The latter point may be explicated with reference to recent work by Jackendoff (1983:19), who develops the position that semantic structures are simply a subset of conceptual structures, "just those conceptual structures that happen to be verbally expressible". Conceptual structure, on Jackendoff's (1983:17) view, is a single level of mental representation at which linguistic, sensory and motor information are compatible. Jackendoff (1983:16) contends that if there were no such level of representation

> it would be impossible to use language to report sensory input. We couldn't talk about what we see and hear. Likewise, there must be a level at which linguistic information is compatible with information eventually conveyed to the motor system, in order to account for our ability to carry out orders and instructions.

He specifically (1983:19) argues that characteristics common to judgments involving visual information, linguistic information and combinations of the two must be accounted for in terms of conceptual structure. And he contends that analogous characteristics arise in judgments of certain fundamental semantic properties of utterances, which are by definition accounted for at the level of semantic structure. On Jackendoff's (1983:19) view "not to treat all these phenomena uniformly would be to miss a crucial generalization about mental computation; hence the semantic and conceptual levels must coincide".[22]

Following Jackendoff, I will assume that the interpretation rule and conceptualization rules postulated in my analysis of the semantics of Afrikaans reduplications specify aspects of conceptual structure. I will therefore pursue the question of the (non-)uniqueness of these rules and principles from this angle. On Jackendoff's (1983:16ff.) theory, there are three types of formal devices involved in the specification of conceptual structure: correspondence rules, conceptual well-formedness rules, and inference and pragmatic rules.

First, correspondence rules have the function of mapping syntactic form directly into conceptual structure. This, clearly, is also the function of the semantic interpretation rule (1), the only difference being that this rule applies to morphological form. Since, within this context, the difference between syntactic and morphological form is inessential, the semantic interpretation rule (1) may be viewed as representing a non-unique type of rule, a correspondence rule. A large number of the semantic interpretation rules that have been proposed in interpretive semantics belong to this type.[23] A typical recent example is the correspondence rule that Jackendoff (1983:181) uses for relating the constituent VP to what he calls "the [ACTION] constituent in conceptual structure":

(60) A VP may be construed as an [ACTION]; the argument position of the verb corresponding to the subject is occupied by the bound variable of the [ACTION].

Second, Jackendoff (1983:17, 22) provides for conceptual well-formedness rules that characterize the possible conceptual structures attainable by human beings. These rules are taken to constitute a finite set of universal and innate devices. Jackendoff (1983:51) assumes that, at a general level, conceptual well-formedness rules specify, for example, that a thing can occupy a place, an event may have a certain number of things and places as parts, and so on. To consider some concrete examples, Jackendoff (1983:162) formulates conceptual well-formedness rules specifying that

(61) "... the place function IN requires its reference object to be regarded as a bounded area or volume ..."

(62) "The most salient place function expressed by "on" requires its reference object to have an upper surface."

On Jackendoff's view (1983:162) it is the violation of the conceptual well-formedness rule (61) that causes The dog is in the dot to be "odd". He points out that the conceptual constraints imposed by (conceptual well-formedness rules for) place functions appear in language as selectional restrictions on the corresponding prepositions. And he (1983:162ff.) proposes a large number of such rules in the formalized format of phrase structure rules.

The rules postulated above for conceptualizing the semantic unit [INCREASED] in conjunction with other semantic units clearly have the same function as Jackendoff's conceptual well-formedness rules. For example, rule (29) specifies that a conceptual constituent made up of the components [INCREASED] and [COUNTABLE THING] will be ill-formed, unless [INCREASED] is conceptualized numerically. And rule (33) specifies, amongst other things, that a conceptual constituent made up of the components [INCREASED] and [TEMPORAL EVENT] will be ill-formed unless [INCREASED] is conceptualized as [INCREASED IN TIME]. These conceptualization rules, thus, are non-unique within a general linguistic context.

Rules or principles with the function of Jackendoff's rules of conceptual well-formedness have been used outside the framework of interpretive semantics by scholars such as Miller and Johnson-Laird (1976:442ff.) - and following them, Lyons (1977:710) - for specifying "the logic of temporal relations". On Lyons's formulation, this "logic of temporal relations ... determines the acceptability of certain combinations of aspectual notions and the unacceptability of others". Such principles are presented implicitly in formulations such as the following by Miller and Johnson-Laird:

(63) (a) "When you arrive somewhere, you stay for a while; when you reach somewhere you may or may not stay. So here is another difference in the temporal shape of verbs." (1976:444)

(b) "Thus BEGIN and END must entail R_t [which is an operator that says merely that the state or process could be observed at some moment - R.P.B.], but they must say something more. A beginning has some sense that the event has not occurred before; an ending that it does not occur thereafter." (1976:449)

On the basis of formulations such as (63)(a) and (b), Lyons (1977:710) reconstructs the principles of Miller and Johnson-Laird's "logic of temporal relations" as follows:

(64) (a) "given the unidimensional directionality of time and our punctual conceptualization of events (i.e. as second-order entities with position, but no magnitude, in the continuum of time), two or more events may be ordered in terms of precedence and successivity, but one event cannot be included, wholly or partly, within another;"

(b) "by virtue of our everyday assumptions about time (notwithstanding our commitment to the theory of relativity), two or more events can be represented as absolutely simultaneous;"

(c) "since states and processes are extended in time, but events are not, an event may be included, as a point, within the temporal extension of a state or process;"

(d) "two (or more) states or processes may be ordered, not only in terms of precedence and successivity, but also in terms of co-extension or (total or partial) inclusion".

Thus, Jackendoff's rules of conceptual well-formedness may be new from the point of view of the theoretical status he assigns to them. In regard to the nature of the claims expressed by them, however, they have precedents in "everyday assumptions" such as those quoted above. This makes the conceptualization rules used in the proposed analysis of Afrikaans reduplication even less unique.[24]

Third, Jackendoff (1983:19, 105) provides for rules of inference and rules of pragmatics that map conceptual structure back onto conceptual structure. He considers the distinction between so-called "semantic" rules of linguistic inference and "pragmatic" rules of linguistic interaction with general knowledge as "less marked than is often supposed". Both kinds are rules for the manipulation of conceptual structure and on Jackendoff's (1983:105) view they "deal with the same primitives and principles of combination". (65) represents a simple and unformalized example of Jackendoff's (1983:73) inference rules.

(65) From the conceptual constituent corresponding to the expression the red hat one may derive the conceptual constituent corresponding to the expression a hat and the conceptual constituent corresponding to something red.

If the term "rule of inference" is restricted to denoting the type of rule exemplified in Jackendoff's discussion such rules appear not to play a role in the semantics of Afrikaans reduplication. It should be noted, however, that the basic ideas embodied in the conceptualization rules proposed above may be expressed by statements that have the purport of "rules of practical inference". Two examples have been formulated as (32') and (37) respectively. The principles constituting Miller and Johnson-Laird's "logic of temporal relations" can also be construed as "rules of practical inference". The question - which cannot be explored here - is to what extent the conceptual well-formedness rules and the rules of inference provided for by Jackendoff belong to mutually exclusive categories of formal devices in terms of function and content.

In sum: the rules postulated in the proposed analysis of the semantics of Afrikaans reduplication do not represent unique kinds of devices that have to be postulated specially for the purpose of this analysis. Such rules have been provided for independently in, for example, Jackendoff's (1983) theory of conceptual structure. It is necessary, though, to note that the interpretation rule and the conceptualization rules of the present analysis do not derive their existence from Jackendoff's overall theory of semantics and cognition. Consequently, shortcomings of the latter theory - such as those discussed by Aitchison (1985) - do not necessarily bear unfavorably on the former rules.

3.15.2 (Non)ad hocness of the individual rules

We come now to the nature of the individual conceptualization rules - (29), (30), (31), (32), (33), (34), (35) (38), (50) and (51) - postulated in preceding sections. It may be contended that these rules are ad hoc in a dual sense, namely in being language-specific, and in taking on the form of stipulations rather than of general lawlike statements.

Consider first the claim that the rules in question are language-specific. This claim entails that only speakers of Afrikaans are mentally equipped with the rules. Thus, taking rule (32) as a typical example, on this claim Afrikaans speakers alone would (be able to) reason in accordance with the idea that for there to be more than one distinct unit of quantity, volume, length, etc. of a specific magnitude, the units have to be nonadjacent, i.e., scattered or distributed in some dimension. Or, turning to rule (34), this claim would entail that unless one were a speaker of Afrikaans one would be incapable of thinking in terms of the idea that a bounded event can occur for an increased time only if it is repeated more than once. Similarly, to be able to think in accordance with rule (38) - which in essence says that the repetition of a nonpunctual event/act indicates its attenuation - one would first have to learn Afrikaans. It would be amazing indeed to find people who, in virtue of their not being native speakers of Afrikaans, could not think in terms of the conceptualization rules under consideration. This, of course, is to reduce to absurdity the claim that the proposed conceptualization rules are ad hoc in the sense of being specific to Afrikaans.

The second claim, viz. that the individual conceptualization rules are ad hoc in having the appearance of stipulations rather than of general lawlike statements, is partially true. This point may be illustrated with reference to rules (29), (33), (40), and (41), repeated here for the sake of convenience as (66), (67), (68) and (69) respectively.

(66) Conceptualize [INCREASED] as [INCREASED IN NUMBER] if it occurs in conjunction with the semantic specification [COUNTABLE THING].

(67) Conceptualize [INCREASED] as [INCREASED IN TIME] if it occurs in conjunction with the semantic unit [TEMPORAL ACT/EVENT].

(68) Conceptualize [INCREASED] as [INCREASED IN INTENSITY]/[INTENSIFIED] if it occurs in conjunction with the semantic unit [VARIABLE/GRADABLE QUALITY].

(69) Conceptualize [INCREASED] as [INCREASED IN SPECIFICITY]/[EMPHASIZED] if it occurs in conjunction with the semantic unit [NONVARIABLE/NONGRADABLE ATTRIBUTE].

Obviously, one would prefer these four rules to follow from one or more general principles of conceptualization. Such a principle or principles would probably subsume the notions "countability (of a thing)", "temporality (of an act)", "variability (of a quality)", and "nonvariability (of an attribute)" under a single unifying concept such as "essential/basic/prime feature (of a thing)".

This, however, is a matter for a broader-based inquiry: it is futile to speculate on the nature and content of such laws on the basis of a study of an area of conceptualization that is restricted to the semantics of one word formation process in one language. To say that the conceptualization rules (66)-(69) have the appearance of stipulations is not to say that they are "artificial" or "contrived". As far as their content is concerned, they have an intuitive naturalness.[25] And, finally, it should be noted that some of the conceptualization rules have only the outward appearance of stipulations. For example, as formulated in (32), repeated below as (70), the conceptualization rule for distribution resembles a stipulation.

(70) Conceptualize [MANY Rs] and [SOME Rs] as respectively [MANY Rs, DISTRIBUTED] and [SOME Rs, DISTRIBUTED] if the former semantic units occur in conjunction with the semantic unit [BOUNDED MEASURE].

But as is clear from (32'), repeated below as (71), rule (32), as far as its basic content is concerned, is anything but a stipulation.

(71) For there to be more than one distinct unit of quantity, volume, length, etc. of a specific magnitude, the units have to be non-adjacent, i.e., scattered or distributed, in some dimension.

Our understanding of semantic and conceptual structure would, however, be significantly extended if <u>all</u> the conceptualization rules postulated in the present study could be reduced to more fundamental principles of conceptualization.

3.15.3 An alternative conception

We have arrived at a natural juncture for considering an alternative conception of the nature of the conceptualization rules under consideration. On this conception these rules would follow from one or more pragmatic principles of conversation and would, consequently, be rules of usage in disguise.

The logical possibility of such a pragmatic conception of the conceptualization rules is suggested by Aronoff's (1980) analysis of the semantics of zero-derived denominal verbs in English.

These verbs (e.g. _to teapot_, _to Rosemary Woods_, _to Houdini_), like evaluative phrases (e.g. _a good nurse_ in _George is a good nurse_) and _-er_ agentives (e.g. _gambler_, _warbler_, _fertilizer_, _reminder_), are so-called "contextuals". That is, in the terminology of Clark and Clark (1979:783), these verbs "... have an indefinitely large number of potential senses, and their interpretation depends on the context, especially the cooperation of the speaker and the listener". Aronoff presents an account of the range of interpretations of new zero-derived verbs in English which differs from Clark and Clark's (1979) analysis in that it neither uses "contextuals" as a new semantic category nor adopts the special convention proposed by Clark and Clark for the interpretation of zero-derived denominal verbs. At the heart of Aronoff's (1980:755) analysis is the conjecture that "... the meaning of a given new word will always be the product of the intersection of an autonomous rule of morphological semantics and pragmatic principles of conversation" (such as Grice's (1975) cooperative principle). And, as a whole, Aronoff's (1980:757) analysis may be viewed as exemplifying "... a method for treating the semantics of morphologically-derived words, wherein a sparse semantics combines with general pragmatic principles in context, to provide a range of interpretations for such words".

Viewed from this perspective, the interpretive rule (1) would represent the "sparse semantics" of Afrikaans reduplication and the conceptualization rules would be disguised formulations of consequences of one or more general pragmatic principles. This conception would derive an _a priori_ measure of attractiveness from the fact that more is known about general pragmatic principles than about general principles of conceptualization. Empirical considerations, however, would disallow an alternative analysis along these pragmatic lines. These empirical considerations derive from the simple fact that Afrikaans reduplications do not have the criterial properties of "contextuals". That is, an arbitrary new Afrikaans reduplication does not have "an infinitely large number of potential senses" (Clark and Clark 1979:783) or "a wide range of possible interpretations" (Aronoff 1980:745) from which one is chosen on a particular occasion in accordance with the context. For example, a new reduplication based on a "numeral" cannot express anything but collectivity or grouping; a new reduplication based on a verb with the aspectual meaning "bounded" can express iteration but not continuation; a new reduplication based on a nongradable adverb can express emphasis only. It is clear that a new Afrikaans reduplication does not have as many potential senses as there are meanings expressible by reduplications in Afrikaans. A new Afrikaans reduplication, thus, is not multiply ambiguous, receiving a particular interpretation in a specific context through the cooperation of the speaker and listener.

To show that it is impossible to reinterpret the proposed conceptualization rules within the pragmatic framework outlined above is not to argue that pragmatic considerations relating to linguistic context, shared knowledge of the speaker and listener, etc. play no role in the interpretation of Afrikaans reduplications. In §3.7 above, it was in fact pointed out that the distinction conventionally drawn between the meanings of "distribution" and "serial ordering" may be reduced in part to differences in the context in which reduplications expressing these meanings occur. For example, kol-kol ("patch patch") may express distribution in either a spatial (= "in (some) scattered patches") or a temporal dimension (= "the one patch after the other"). That the former interpretation has to be chosen in the case of (72) and the latter in the case of (73) is indicated by the different linguistic contexts.

(72) Die gras is kol - kol aan die brand.
the grass is patch patch on the burn
"The grass is burning in scattered patches."

(73) Soos dit warmer word, sal die gras <u>kol - kol</u>
as it hotter become will the grass patch patch
verdroog.
wither
"As it becomes hotter, the grass will wither in one patch after the other."

In these sentences the pragmatic variable of context thus co-determines the choice of a specific interpretation for a potentially ambiguous distributive reduplication.[26] The distributivity reading itself, however, is a function of the interaction of the meaning [INCREASED], as specified by the interpretation rule (1), and the semantic specification [BOUNDED MEASURE] in the dictionary entry for the lexical base <u>kol</u>. As far as I can see, this interaction cannot be captured in pragmatic terms without reducing such notions as "pragmatic" and "context" to contentless labels.

3.16 Retrospect

Here now are the main findings of the preceding analysis of the semantics of Afrikaans reduplication(s):

1. For some understanding to be gained of the semantics of Afrikaans reduplication, a distinction has to be drawn between the information conveyed by the process of reduplication and the total information content associated with reduplications as products of this process.
2. As a formal means, reduplication expresses one unit of semantic content only, namely [INCREASED] - a unit that has to be amalgamated with the unit of meaning of the base form that is being reduplicated.
3. The unit of semantic content [INCREASED] is assigned by the interpretation rule (1) (= Interpret $[\alpha_i \alpha_i]$ as [A INCREASED] where A represents the sense or meaning of α and [INCREASED] represents an abstract semantic unit) to all reduplications generated by the formation rule (2) of §2.1 ($= \alpha_i \rightarrow \alpha_i \alpha_i$). The former interpretation rule instantiates Jackendoff's correspondence rules.

4. The various meanings, i.e. composites of total information content, assigned to Afrikaans reduplications in conventional studies are functions of the interaction between the interpretation rule (1) and other, independent, conceptual devices.
5. By the application of four conceptualization rules the semantic unit [INCREASED], as assigned by rule (1), is variously conceptualized as follows:
   (a) as [INCREASED IN NUMBER] if the meaning of the base form includes the semantic unit [COUNTABLE THING];
   (b) as [INCREASED IN TIME] if the meaning of the base form includes the semantic unit [TEMPORAL EVENT/ACT];
   (c) as [INCREASED IN INTENSITY] if the meaning of the base form includes the semantic unit [VARIABLE/GRADABLE QUALITY];
   (d) as [INCREASED IN SPECIFICITY] if the meaning of the base form includes the semantic unit [NON-VARIABLE/ NONGRADABLE ATTRIBUTE].

   These conceptualization rules resemble Jackendoff's conceptual well-formedness rules and will hopefully turn out to be consequences of a single more fundamental principle of conceptualization.
6. The distinction between the meanings "considerable number" and "limited number" is a function of the differing semantic contributions of a plural affix to the lexical meanings of base forms.
7. The meanings "distribution" and "serial ordering" are both yielded by a conceptualization rule which says that, for there to be more than one unit of quantity, volume, length, etc. of a given magnitude, the units must be thought of as scattered in some dimension.
8. The distinction between the meanings "distribution" and "serial ordering" reduces to a difference between the dimensions in which the measure units are scattered: a spatial dimension in the case of "distribution" as opposed to a temporal or logical dimension in the case of "serial ordering", the choice of interpretation in

the case of a specific utterance being codetermined by pragmatic considerations.

9. The meaning "collectivity/grouping" derives from the semantic specification [NUMERICAL GROUP] that forms part of the dictionary entry of certain base forms.
10. The meaning "iteration" is formed by means of a conceptualization rule which says that, when it occurs in conjunction with the aspectual unit [BOUNDED EVENT/ACT], the unit of meaning [INCREASED IN TIME] is conceptualized as [REPEATED].
11. The meaning "continuation" is formed by the application of a conceptualization rule which says that, when it occurs in conjunction with the aspectual unit [UNBOUNDED EVENT/ACT], the unit of content [INCREASED IN TIME] has to be conceptualized as [CONTINUED].
12. The meaning "attenuation" is formed by the application of a conceptualization rule which says that, when it occurs in conjunction with the aspectual unit [NONPUNCTUAL], the unit of content [REPEATED] can be conceptualized as [REPEATED AND ATTENUATED].
13. In these terms, therefore, the distinction between "iteration", "continuation" and "attenuation" reduces to aspectual differences between verb bases.
14. The distinction between the meanings "intensity" and "emphasis" derives from a more fundamental distinction in the semantic specification of adjectives/ adverbs, namely the distinction between [VARIABLE/ GRADABLE QUALITY] and [NONVARIABLE/NONGRADABLE ATTRIBUTE].
15. Consequently the interpretation rule (1) for reduplication need not account directly for any of the meanings conventionally characterized as "considerable number", "limited number", "distribution", "serial ordering", "collectivity/grouping", "iteration", "continuation", "attenuation", "intensity", and "emphasis".

These findings provide further illustration of the heuristic power of the Galilean style. The pursuit of depth of insight has led us to the postulation of a single strongly unifying interpretation rule that applies to all Afrikaans reduplications. This rule expresses the strong claim that Afrikaans reduplication is a simple, unitary phenomenon from a semantic point of view too. And in motivating and defending this rule, a variety of observations and beliefs about the (apparent diversity of the) meanings of Afrikaans reduplications have been found to lack the factual status conventionally accorded to them.

3.17 Consequences

Let us next consider two language-specific consequences and four general-linguistic consequences of the preceding analysis of the semantics of Afrikaans reduplication.

3.17.1 Language-specific consequences

A first language-specific consequence of the analysis has already been noted: the semantics of Afrikaans reduplication is extremely simple. The information expressed by Afrikaans reduplication is captured by the single interpretation rule (1) that is both simple and general. As has been argued in some detail, the conventional view that Afrikaans reduplication expresses a wide array of highly specific meanings stems from a failure to draw a distinction between the semantic unit associated with the process of reduplication and the total information content of individual reduplications. It is the latter content that is subject to variation.

A second language-specific consequence of the analysis is perhaps less obvious. In terms of the basic device of the analysis, the interpretation rule (1), the fundamental unit of meaning expressed by Afrikaans reduplication is [INCREASED]. A range of other units of meaning are formed on the basis of this fundamental unit by the conceptualization rules.

These "secondary" units - e.g., [CONSIDERABLE NUMBER], [DISTRIBUTED], [ATTENUATED], etc. - are therefore in a clear sense derived units. The reverse cannot be excluded on a priori grounds, however. For example, [DISTRIBUTED] could have been the fundamental unit of meaning associated with Afrikaans reduplication and [INCREASED] a derived unit. In fact, such a state of affairs does not appear to be impossible in language in general. Gil (1982:202ff.) has argued that the fundamental "meaning" associated with reduplication in Georgian is "distributivity".[27] Why then should [INCREASED], rather than [DISTRIBUTED], be the fundamental semantic unit expressed by reduplication in Afrikaans?

The essence of the answer to this question is as follows: if [DISTRIBUTED] were taken as the fundamental semantic unit expressed by reduplication in Afrikaans and [INCREASED] as a derived unit, it would be impossible to provide a simple and unified account of the semantics of Afrikaans reduplication. Thus, suppose that (74) rather than (1) were taken as the basic semantic interpretation rule for Afrikaans reduplication.

(74) Interpret $[\alpha_i \alpha_i]$ as [A DISTRIBUTED]
(where A represents the meaning of α and DISTRIBUTED represents an abstract semantic unit)

If the rule (74) were applied in conjunction with appropriate conceptualization rules, it could be made to "work" in the case of a number of the meanings conventionally associated with Afrikaans reduplications. Thus, applied in conjunction with a conceptualization rule such as (75), the interpretation rule (74) could be used to account for the meanings characterized conventionally as "considerable number" ("many Rs") and "limited number" ("some Rs").

(75) Conceptualize [DISTRIBUTED] as [DISTRIBUTED AND INCREASED IN NUMBER] if it occurs in conjunction with the semantic unit [COUNTABLE THING].

This rule would express the idea that countable things could be distributed only if they were multiplied at the same time. Given the interpretation rule (74) and the conceptualization rule (75), the total information content of reduplications such as bottels-bottels (= "bottles bottles") in (2)(a), bakke-bakke (= "bowls bowls") in (2)(b), ent-ent (= "stretch stretch") in (3)(a) and ruk-ruk (= "time time") in (3)(b) could be accounted for.

However, if (74) were taken as the basic interpretation rule, it would become impossible to account for meanings such as those characterized conventionally as "intensity" ("very

R") and "emphasis" ("emphatically, etc., ... R"). As far as I can see, [DISTRIBUTED] does not constitute a component of the latter meanings at all. This would entail that the rule (74) would have to be prevented, in some essentially ad hoc manner, from applying to reduplications such as dik-dik (= "thick thick") in (13)(a), amper-amper (= "nearly nearly") in (13)(b), hier-hier (= "here here") in (14)(a) and saam-saam (= "together together") in (14)(b). It would also entail that, in addition to (74), other interpretation rules would have to be postulated for specifying the meanings of these reduplications. To consider [DISTRIBUTED] the fundamental unit of content expressed by reduplication in Afrikaans, therefore, would make it impossible to give a simple and unifying account of the semantics of this process. It has been shown above that such an account can be given if [INCREASED], rather than [DISTRIBUTED], is taken to be the fundamental unit of meaning expressed by reduplication in Afrikaans.

Notice that the semantic unit [INCREASED] can be expressed in Afrikaans by means other than reduplication. It may be expressed, for example, by the quantifier meer (= "more") in the case of nouns, verbs, adjectives and adverbs, as is clear from the (b) sentences below.

(76) *Nouns*

(a) Die kinders drink bottels-bottels limonade.
The children drink bottles bottles lemonade
"The children drink bottles and bottles of lemonade."

(b) Die kinders drink meer bottels limonade as voorheen.
The children drink more bottles lemonade than before
"The children are consuming more bottles of lemonade than before."

(77) *Verbs*

(a) Hy lek - lek oor sy droë lippe.
he lick lick over his dry lips
"He licks and relicks his dry lips."

(b) Hy lek meer oor sy droë lippe as wat goed is.
he lick more over his dry lips than what good is
"He licks his dry lips more than is good for them."

(78) *Adjectives*

(a) Dit is 'n eensame-eensame lot wat op hom wag.
it is a lonely lonely fate which on him wait
"It is a more lonely fate than he expected."

(b) Dit is 'n meer eensame lot as wat hy verwag het.
it is a more lonely fate than what he expect has
"It is a more lonely fate than he expected."

(79) *Adverbs*

(a) Die dae rek geleidelik-geleidelik in die lente.
the days lengthen gradually gradually in the spring
"The days lengthen only very gradually in spring."

(b) Die dae rek meer geleidelik in die lente,
the days lengthen more gradually in the spring
as in die somer.
than in the summer
"The days lengthen more gradually in spring than in summer."

But this is what one would expect. If [INCREASED] were indeed a fundamental semantic unit, as was claimed by our semantic analysis, it would be rather peculiar if reduplication were the only means of expressing it. Thus, the fact that [INCREASED] may be expressed by the quantifier meer, together with the fact that meer cuts across the lexical categories that may be reduplicated, provides indirect evidence of an independent sort for the fundamental status assigned to this semantic unit.[28]

3.17.2 General-linguistic consequences

A first general-linguistic consequence of our analysis of the semantics of Afrikaans reduplication concerns the nature of the relationship between morphological form and semantic representation. The relationship between the interpretation rule (1) of §3.1 and the formation rule (2) of §2.1 is quite direct, as has been suggested by expressions such as "the unit of meaning/information expressed by reduplication in Afrikaans". Lexicalist morphologists who have argued that the semantic aspect of word formation is autonomous from its formal or structural aspect may object to the use of these expressions. Some may construe the directness of the relationship between the formation rule and the interpretation rule as representing a violation of the so-called autonomy thesis, formulated as follows by Lieber (1981:65):

(80) The "syntactic" or structural aspect of word formation should be autonomous from lexical semantics.[29]

But objections such as these would miss the point that reduplication is a special means of word formation: a means of word formation that involves a form of iconicity. This form of iconicity entails that form and meaning resemble each other in a quantitative respect: an increase in form corresponds with an increase in the projected referent(s) of the form.[30] A formation rule such as (2) of §2.1, therefore, is motivated in a Saussurean sense. Against this background it makes sense to say that "reduplication expresses the unit of meaning [INCREASED]". The directness of the relationship between the formation rule (2) and the interpretation rule (1), consequently, does not represent a real violation of the autonomy thesis (80). Rather, the directness of this relationship indicates that the autonomy thesis (80) has to be restricted in scope to word formation that does not involve iconicity.

A second general-linguistic consequence of the semantic analysis under consideration bears on the question of the (lexical) category status of the constituents of Afrikaans reduplications. In §2.7 above, it was noted that lexicalist morphologists have implicitly assumed that the constituents of morphologically complex words retain the (lexical) category status that they have as independent forms. It was observed, however, that it is difficult to find formal evidence for this assumption, the so-called Category Retention Constraint (118) of §2.7. Recall that the constituents of a reduplication such as <u>ent-ent</u> (= "stretch stretch") do not have the formal properties that would warrant assignment of the category status Noun to them. This raised the question of whether there were phonological and/or semantic interpretation rules whose formulation required that these constituents, namely $\underline{ent}_1$ and $\underline{ent}_2$, be assigned the status of Noun.

The semantic interpretation rule (1) and the conceptualization rules have been formulated informally only. Consequently, one cannot draw particularly firm conclusions of a general sort from these formulations. Keeping this in mind, notice that neither in the formulation of the semantic interpretation rule, nor in that of the conceptualization rules, was it necessary to refer to the lexical category of the bases of the relevant reduplications. Thus, these rules and principles do not provide any grounds for assigning $\underline{ent}_1$ and $\underline{ent}_2$ the status of Noun or, more generally, for accepting the Category Retention Constraint.[31]

A third general consequence of the preceding analysis of the semantics of Afrikaans reduplications concerns the issue of the kinds of entities to which linguistic expressions may refer in the projected world. As has been noted in §3.3 above, Jackendoff (1983:48) argues that these entities are not, as has traditionally been assumed, restricted to the ontological category "thing", but may also belong to other ontological categories - including "place", "direction", "action", "event", "manner". This assumption of a diversity of ontological categories to which linguistic expressions may refer receives some support from the preceding analysis of the semantics of Afrikaans reduplication. Without assuming that bases of Afrikaans reduplications may refer to things as well as to events, acts, processes, qualities and attributes, it would not be possible to formulate a single unifying interpretation rule such as (1). By applying the interpretation rule (1) to conceptual constituents of the category "thing", "event", "act", "process", "quality" and "attribute", the claim is expressed that these constituents share a fundamental feature, namely "increasability". This yields some support for analyses that have attempted to capture intuitively perceived semantic correspondences among linguistic forms belonging to distinct formal categories such as nouns, verbs, adjectives and adverbs. The preceding analysis also provides some evidence that "boundedness" represents one of the parameters common to the semantics of such categorially distinct linguistic forms. This is clear from the role that the semantic unit [BOUNDED] has played in the formulation of the conceptualization rules (32), (34), (35), (40), and (41).[32]

A fourth general consequence of the preceding analysis of the semantics of Afrikaans reduplication is of a methodological rather than a substantive sort. It concerns the adequacy of conventional analyses of the semantics of reduplication in languages and creoles other than Afrikaans. As evidenced by Moravscik's (1978) survey, these analyses characterize the "meaning(s)" or "semantic function(s)" of reduplication in terms of notions such as "considerable/limited quantity/number", "serial ordering", "collectivity", "distribution", "distributive plurality", "iteration", "continuation", "attenuation", "intensity", etc. as if these notions represented atomic units without any internal structure. Such studies, therefore, fail to draw a systematic distinction between, on the one hand, the semantic unit(s) which reduplication contributes to the total information content of reduplications and, on the other hand, the units of information contributed to this total content by other factors, including lexical meaning, aspectual meaning, and conceptualization rules. As a result, a wildly diverse array of meanings are claimed to be associated with the formal process of reduplication. Consider in this respect Moravscik's (1978:325) conclusion that "Given that reduplication is neither the exclusive expression of any one meaning category in languages, nor are the meanings that it is an expression of all subsumable under general classes, no explanatory or predictive generalization about the meanings of reduplicative constructions can be proposed." It may be true that reduplication expresses different meanings in different languages or even in one and the same language. This, however, cannot be established by subjecting languages to a superficial taxonomic or survey-type analysis that is performed outside the framework of an explanatory semantic theory.[33] The diversity of meanings attributed to reduplication as a formal process by conventional studies may, on closer inspection, turn out to be a function of the failure of such studies to draw the necessary conceptual distinctions. This is suggested by the history of the study of Afrikaans reduplication.

4 Link-up

This chapter provides further clarification of the manner in which the proposed theories of the formation and interpretation of Afrikaans reduplications are linked. The formation rule (2) of §2.1 copies all nouns (including cardinals), verbs, adjectives and adverbs, subject to the general constraints presented in Chapter 2 above. To each reduplication formed by this rule, the interpretation rule (1) of §3.1 assigns the semantic unit [INCREASED A]. This semantic unit is developed further by the conceptualization rules proposed in Chapter 3 above.

Note that the formation rule and the interpretation rule jointly generate a large number of reduplications that are unacceptable to native speakers. A significant subset of these unacceptable reduplications, being conceptually ill-formed, are filtered out by the conceptualization rules. That is, a subset of the reduplications generated jointly by the formation and interpretation rules are formally well-formed, but are unacceptable because the concepts corresponding to them are characterized as ill-formed by the conceptualization rules. The projected referents of such reduplications cannot be conceptualized in a coherent manner on these rules.[1]

A few examples may serve to illustrate the filtering function of the conceptualization rules.

(1) (a) *Hy woon in <u>Parys-Parys</u>.
he live in Paris Paris
"*He is living in a number of Parises."

(b) *Sorg-sorg is hier nodig.
care care is here required
"*Scattered care is required here."

(c) *Hy woon-woon in Parys.
he live live in Paris
"*He continually lives in Paris."

(d) *Net die ryker - ryker mense
only the rich + COMPAR rich + COMPAR people
kan gaan.
can go
"*Only the very richer people can go."

(e) *Hy kweek mooier - mooier proteas.
he grow lovely + COMPAR lovely + COMPAR proteas
"*He grows very lovelier proteas."

The reduplication Parys-Parys (= "Paris Paris") in (1)(a) is unacceptable because its conceptualization requires a rule that would provide for a conceptual state of affairs in which more than one of a unique entity could exist. Less informally, there is no conceptualization rule stating that [INCREASED] may be conceptualized as [INCREASED IN NUMBER] in conjunction with a semantic unit, [PARIS], that has the component [UNIQUE PLACE]. Hence the conceptualization rules of Chapter 3 assign no conceptual structure to Parys-Parys and, in this way, predict that this reduplication will be unacceptable. A similar account can be given for the unacceptability of the other reduplications in (1)(b)-(e). Informally: (i) in the case of sorg-sorg ("care care") there is no rule for conceptualizing an unbounded entity as scattered in some dimension, (ii) in the case of woon-woon (= "live live") there is no rule for conceptualizing a habitual activity as being performed continually (on such a rule a tautology would be conceptually well-formed), (iii) in the case of ryker-ryker (= "richer richer") and mooier-mooier ("lovelier lovelier") there is no rule for conceptualizing a "comparative" property as intensified in such a way that it retains its "comparativeness" and does not become a "superlative" property.

Note that the conceptual ill-formedness of ryker-ryker and mooier-mooier clarifies a remark made in §2.3 above about the category type of the bases of Afrikaans reduplications. It was observed that these reduplications can be based on inflected forms, but that not all reduplications based on inflected forms will necessarily be acceptable. As has been shown with reference to ryker-ryker and mooier-mooier, reduplications to which the conceptualization rules fail to assign a (well-formed) conceptual structure will be unacceptable. The conceptualization rules, then, allow us to uphold the claim that morphologically complex words can be reduplicated, without there being any need to append quasi-formal qualifications to this claim. This is a fortunate outcome since a qualification stating that comparatives, inflected with -er, cannot be reduplicated has no explanatory power whatsoever. Conceptual ill-formedness, then, is a cause of the deviance of a significant class of unacceptable Afrikaans reduplications.

It is not claimed, however, that conceptualization rules can be invoked to explain the deviance of all unacceptable reduplications. To see this, contrast the unacceptability of the reduplication in sentence (2)(b) with the acceptability of the one in (2)(a).

(2) (a) Sy ondersteuners kom vyf - vyf om afskeid
his supporters come five five to leave
te neem.
to take
"His supporters are coming to take their leave in groups of five."

(b) *Sy ondersteuners kom [sewe - en - dertig duisend
his supporters come seven and thirty thousand
nege honderd vyf - en - tagtig]-[sewe - en -
nine hundred five and eighty seven and
dertig duisend nege honderd vyf - en - tagtig] om
thirty thousand nine hundred five and eighty to
afskeid te neem.
leave to take
"His supporters are coming to take their leave in groups of thirty seven thousand nine hundred and eighty five."

The formation rule (2) of §2.1 generates the reduplication in (2)(b) as one of the infinitely many reduplications based on so-called cardinals. And the unit of meaning [INCREASED] is assigned to this reduplication by the interpretation rule (1) of §3.1. Since the meaning of the nonreduplicated base of the reduplication incorporates the semantic unit [GROUP] of which [COUNTABLE THING] is a component, the conceptualization rules (29) and (32) of Chapter 3 assign a well-formed conceptual structure to the reduplication. This structure may be represented informally as "in one group of thirty seven thousand nine hundred and eighty five after the other". The unacceptability of this reduplication therefore cannot be attributed to conceptual ill-formedness. Neither can it be ascribed to a purely formal factor, seeing that vyf, as base of the reduplication in (2)(a), and sewe-en-dertig duisend nege honderd vyf-en-tagtig, as base of the reduplication in (2)(b), do not differ in any formal respect that is relevant to the statement of word formation rules.

In addition to differing in acceptability, the reduplications in (2)(a) and (b) obviously differ in complexity as well. There is, first of all, a difference in phonological complexity: the reduplication in (2)(a), which consists of two syllables, is phonologically much less complex than the one in (2)(b), which consists of thirty syllables. At a deeper level this difference is possibly associated with a difference in perceptual complexity. Note also that the phonological complexity of the second reduplication may be incompatible with the condition that reduplications must form prosodic units, that is, they must be pronounced as units, at a relatively fast tempo. The two reduplications, moreover, differ in morphological complexity: the one in (2)(a) consists of two morphologically simple words, whereas the one in (2)(b) consists of two compounded "cardinals" that have a quite complex internal morphological structure. This difference too may cause the second reduplication to be perceptually much more complex and to make much higher demands on short term memory than the first.

All of this indicates that it cannot be demanded on *a priori* grounds that the theory of formation and the theory of interpretation should account for the deviance of every unacceptable reduplication. These theories, obviously, have to form part of a more comprehensive network that comprises theories of phonetic interpretation, speech perception and production, memory storage and retrieval, etc. The observed differences between the reduplications in (2)(a) and (2)(b) may well serve as an indication of the kinds of constraints to be imposed by the latter theories on the acceptability of Afrikaans reduplications. Discovering what these constraints are must be the subject of a separate study, however.

5 Metascientific retrospection

The metascientific concern of this study has been to provide an illustration of the heuristic power of the Galilean style. Specifically, this concern has been with showing that this mode of inquiry may be profitably used to pursue depth of insight in less well researched areas, such as morphology and semantics, too. Given the characterization of this style presented in Chapter 1, the proposed analyses of the formation and interpretation of Afrikaans reduplications are clearly Galilean in nature. These analyses are Galilean in essentially two, complementary, respects: in their pursuit of theoretical unification, and in their treatment of data or "facts" that appear to pose a threat to unifying principles.

Consider first the manner in which the analyses illustrate the Galilean pursuit of depth of understanding through theoretical unification. Both the analysis of the formation and that of the interpretation of Afrikaans reduplications yielded strongly unifying theories. The theory of formation derives its unifying power from the single formation rule formulated as (2) in Chapter 2 and the various general constraints to which this rule was made subject. As regards the formation rule, it says in effect that all Afrikaans reduplications are formed in the same way, regardless of the lexical category to which these reduplications and their bases belong. To postulate only one formation rule for all Afrikaans reduplications is to say that from the point of view of their formation, these forms manifest a unitary phenomenon. As noted above, the general constraints placed on this rule constitute the second source of unifying power of the theory of formation. In being both rule-type independent and language-independent, these constraints represent truly unifying principles of word formation. By invoking constraints that are rule-type independent, the theory of formation says that Afrikaans reduplications are formed in fundamentally the same way as other morphologically complex forms such as compounds and derived words. And by invoking constraints that are also language-independent, the theory achieves even greater unification. It says in effect that Afrikaans reduplications are formed like morphologically complex words in language in general. In sum then: the theory of formation is strongly unifying in claiming that all Afrikaans reduplications are formed by one and the same rule, that Afrikaans reduplications are formed in fundamentally the same way as other types of Afrikaans complex words, and that Afrikaans reduplications are formed in fundamentally the same way as morphologically complex words in language in general.

The theory of the interpretation of Afrikaans reduplications, too, achieves a considerable measure of unification. In postulating only one interpretation rule, namely (1) of Chapter 3, it says that as far as meaning is concerned, Afrikaans reduplication is a unitary phenomenon: all reduplications express the same meaning, regardless of differences in form that may exist among them. By postulating language-independent conceptualization rules in addition to the interpretation rule, the theory unifies the interpretation of Afrikaans reduplications with that of linguistic expressions in language in general. The theory says in effect that as regards meaning or conceptual structure, Afrikaans reduplications obey the same well-formedness constraints as linguistic expressions in language in general. And by using such conceptualization rules the theory assimilates the interpretation of Afrikaans reduplications to principles of cognition in general. In sum: the theory of interpretation is strongly unifying in claiming that all Afrikaans reduplications express the same basic meaning, that this meaning may be expressed by a single rule, that this meaning may be further conceptualized in the same way as those of linguistic expressions in language in general, and that this conceptualization conforms to general principles of cognition.

This brings us to the second respect in which the proposed analyses of the formation and interpretation of Afrikaans reduplications are Galilean in nature. In the pursuit of theoretical unification, be it in natural science or linguistics, many apparently recalcitrant phenomena are encountered. One of the salient characteristics of the Galilean style is the way in which the so-called negative data or "facts" derived from apparently recalcitrant phenomena are dealt with. When such data are encountered, the first reaction is not to abandon potentially unifying theories on which the data appear to bear. Rather, apparently negative data are reanalyzed and an attitude of epistemological tolerance is adopted towards the threatened theories for as long as the exact import of these data remains unclear. The analyses of the interpretation and formation of Afrikaans reduplications provide ample illustration of this feature of the Galilean style. Thus, both analyses are upheld in the face of an extensive range of data that, unless they are reanalyzed as proposed, appear to bear negatively on the unifying principles on which these analyses hinge. For example, in the morphological analysis Afrikaans cardinals were reanalyzed as nouns in order to retain the Open Category Constraint (39) in §2.5. And to uphold the Endocentricity Constraint (45) in §2.6 as a promising unifying principle, a whole range of so-called exocentric reduplications were reanalyzed either as endocentric reduplications or as nonreduplicated morphologically complex words. Likewise, to uphold the semantic analysis a whole range of data that appeared to bear negatively on the unifying interpretation rule were reanalyzed. For example, meanings assumed by conventional analyses to be atomic were reanalyzed as composite; and meanings that are conventionally construed as basic were reanalyzed as derived.

The morphological and semantic reanalyses presented in the preceding sections share two notable features. These reanalyses were motivated by the fact that, in every case, the apparent recalcitrance of the data posing a threat to the proposed unifying principles was found to be a function of arbitrary or untenable assumptions made by conventional analyses of Afrikaans reduplication. And the empirical justification for the claims about Afrikaans expressed by these reanalyses is much stronger than the justification provided for the claims of conventional studies. That is, rather than showing a disregard for the so-called facts of Afrikaans, the proposed reanalyses have unmasked certain "facts" as fictions and, moreover, have uncovered numerous new facts about the language. This amounts to saying that the pursuit of theoretical unification is a powerful heuristic strategy which not only yields deeper theoretical understanding but also leads to increased factual accuracy.

Notes

1 Introduction

1. For some discussion of these simplified registers and of the status of reduplication in them cf., e.g., Ferguson and DeBose 1977. For some of the functions of reduplication in pidgins cf. Todd 1974:19-20.

2. Thus, Bouman (1939:346) states that "Het Afrikaans kent reduplicatie-formaties op een in het overige Indogermaans ongehoorde schaal, met verchillende functies. Het principe is zózeer deel geworden van de inwendige vorm der taal, dat het volledig produktief is gebleven."

3. For references to studies that have argued for versions of this position cf. Raidt 1980:496, 1981:182.

4. According to Raidt (1981:187) Afrikaans reduplication is based on both the Dutch and the Malay pattern. She claims that Malay forms strengthened existing Dutch reduplication "tendencies" and that Dutch, in addition, took over new "un-Dutch" forms of reduplication from Malay.

5. Because of the reservations alluded to above - namely that the expression "the Galilean style" should be used symbolically rather than literally and that its historical implications should not be taken too seriously - it would perhaps be more appropriate to call this style of inquiry "the lax Galilean style of (linguistic) inquiry", as I have done elsewhere (Botha 1982:42). The expression "the Galilean style", however, has been generally used by linguists and I will do so too - always, however, with the above-mentioned reservations. Botha (1982) presents a detailed critical appraisal of Chomsky's (1980) characterization of the Galilean style. The literature contains a variety of misconceptions of Chomsky's use of this style of inquiry. One of the most misunderstood aspects of this style is the thesis (2)(d) of epistemological tolerance. Thus, this thesis has been criticized as an objectionable means that allows Chomsky to disregard refuting evidence and to arbitrarily confine his inquiry to those (restricted) areas in which his theories "work". Sinclair's (1985) analysis of the rationality of Chomsky's linguistics, and Botha and Sinclair's (to appear) critical discussion of Brame's (1985) reconstruction of Chomsky's

thesis of epistemological tolerance show how off-target these criticisms have been.

2 Formation

1. For some discussion of the general properties assigned to words by theories of lexicalist morphology, cf., e.g., Aronoff 1976:1, 7, 8-10, 17-20, Lieber 1981:1, Selkirk 1982:1-9, Thomas-Flinders 1983:3-11. For general characterizations of a more traditional sort of a notion of "the word", cf., e.g., Adams 1973:7-8, Bauer 1983:7-10.

2. This constraint is formulated in a slightly different manner in Botha 1980:116, 1981:46. For an appeal by a more orthodox lexicalist morphologist to what appears to be the essence of the constraint cf. Allen 1978:112-3. Like Aronoff (1976:2), who was following Postal (1969), Selkirk (1982:53) also extends the scope of a version of this constraint so as to include rules that establish anaphoric relations. And recently Simpson (1983:2) has formulated an aspect of this constraint as the so-called Lexical Integrity Hypothesis, which states that syntactic processes cannot look into the internal structure of words. The constraint (5) has figured also in various forms in nonlexicalist theories of word formation, as is clear from Adams's (1973:8ff.) discussion of the "rule of uninterruptibility" that lies at the basis of the conventional distinction between words and syntactic phrases.

3. In presenting Afrikaans data, I will generally
   (a) provide both a literal gloss and more idiomatic translation when citing an Afrikaans form for the first time, but in subsequent citations will often give the literal gloss alone;
   (b) represent relevant affixes in capitals where this may assist the reader in "processing" the data;
   (c) use the plus sign '+' to indicate the boundary between an affix and the base to which it is attached, and that between the constituents of a compound;
   (d) use the minus sign '-' to indicate the boundary between the constituents of a reduplication, and
   (e) use the square brackets '[]' to indicate constituency in cases that lend themselves to misunderstanding.

4. For observations on the phonetic differences between reduplications and lexically related syntactic phrases in Afrikaans cf., e.g., Scholtz 1963:149, Raidt 1981:178.

5. Among the lexicalists who have adopted one or another version of this constraint are Allen (1978:4, 253), Roeper and Siegel (1978:202), and Selkirk (1982:8).

6. Lexicalist morphologists disagree about the extension to be assigned to the term "word" within this constraint. Aronoff (1976:4) and Kiparsky (1982:22-3), for example, have restricted it to "actual" or "existing" words only, whereas Allen (1978:185), for example, has extended it so as to include "possible" words as well.

7. This constraint cannot be correct in its full generality, a point to which I will return in §2.11 below.

8. Within Moravscik's (1978:304-5) framework, this generalization may be captured by a constraint of lexical identity: the copy and copied constituent must be identical instances (tokens) of the same lexical form (type). Within her (1978:304) framework, moreover, Afrikaans reduplication would be "total reduplication" in the sense that it involved the "iteration" of the whole string "whose meaning was correspondingly changed". And within Moravscik's framework, Afrikaans reduplication would be "bimodal" in the sense that the "constituents to be reduplicated", i.e., the bases, had to be "defined" with reference to both their "meaning properties" and their "sound properties".

9. For the first aspect of this interrelatedness cf. (15) above.

10. For a characterization of the notion of "open category/class" and of the complementary notion of "closed category/class" cf., e.g., Gleason 1965:189, Pike 1967:201, Quirk et al. 1972:46, Lyons 1977:155-6.

11. For some discussion of the devices by which these kinds of new words are created in English cf. Marchand 1969.

12. Many of the reduplications presented below are found in Kempen 1969.

13. The former nouns, in turn, may be related by means of zero affixation, conversion or lexical redundancy to the verbs <u>strum</u> and <u>uff</u>:

 Hy <u>strum</u> die ghitaar.
 he <u>strum</u> the guitar
 "He strums the guitar."
 Hy <u>uff</u> gerusstellend.
 he <u>uff</u> reassuringly
 "He grunts reassuringly."

14. Cf. also Romaine 1983:178 for this constraint, where it is called a "principle".

15. Within a recent version of Chomsky's (1981:48) Revised Extended Standard Theory, N, V and A still have the status of lexical categories and P is still considered not to be a lexical category. Within this theory, Chomsky (1981:252, 272) uses the notion "lexical category" to delimit the set of proper governors: only lexical categories can be proper governors. On Radford's (1981:319) interpretation, this use of the notion "lexical category" indicates that Chomsky has modified the <u>Aspects</u> notion of "lexical category" in an essential respect. For a conception of lexical categories that differs from Chomsky's latest cf. Bresnan 1982:295.

16. For one way in which a distinction may be drawn within a lexicalist framework between rules of zero affixation, conversion and lexical redundancy cf. Lieber 1981:chapter

3. Cf. also Jackendoff 1975 and Aronoff 1976:30-1 for a distinction between WFRs and lexical redundancy rules. Aronoff (1982) has recently argued against the use of non-directional rules of derivation, specifically as these figure within Lieber's theory of the lexicon.

17. Kiparsky (1982:6) includes both lexical categories and features like Transitive and Agent in the scope of the constraint.

18. As was noted above, the list of so-called exocentric types of reduplication does not include types that have been claimed to be unproductive. For example, it excludes adjectival reduplications which on Kempen's (1969:228) analysis are claimed to be based on nouns. Kempen presents only two examples of this type:

    Die pad is vreeslik gat - gat.
    the road is terribly hole hole
    "The road is terribly holed/full of holes."
    Hoekom is jou lippe so rand-rand vanmôre?
    why are your lips so rim rim this morning
    "Why are your lips so rimmed this morning?"

As a further example of an unproductive allegedly exocentric type of reduplication one may consider the verbs cited by Kempen (1969:139) as due to adjective reduplication:

    Hy bleek-bleek.
    he pale pale
    "He turns pale (as death?)"
    Hy wou die saak sommer blou-blou.
    he wanted the matter just blue blue
    "He wanted to let the matter rest."

Forms such as gat-gat, rand-rand, bleek-bleek and blou-blou may be listed in the lexicon - if native speakers judge them acceptable. Being finite in number, and perhaps deviant as well, they obviously do not evidence the existence of processes that should be accounted for by means of rules.

19. For the structural configuration in which measure phrases in predicate position occur in English cf. Jackendoff 1977:140.

20. Transformations, by contrast, are exceptionless on Wasow's view.

21. The possibility is not being excluded, of course, that such exceptions may be accounted for in terms of non-formal considerations - e.g. considerations of a semantic, pragmatic, logical, or conceptual sort.

22. For some of the properties associated in conventional analyses with adverbs that occur in the post-verbal predicate position cf. Kempen 1969:70.

23. For the use of lexical redundancy rules as devices to account for morphological (word formation) phenomena cf.,

e.g., Jackendoff 1975, Aronoff 1976:31, Wasow 1977, Lieber 1981:126, and Kiparsky 1983:6ff.

24. The analysis of such reduplications as stywebeen-stywebeen presented above was based on Kempen's and Theron's claim that many lexical items in Afrikaans are members of both the category Noun and the category Adverb. Suppose, however, for the sake of argument, that this claim were false. Suppose, specifically, that in sentences such as (74)(b) and (75)(b) stywebeen and witpens in post-verbal position did not have the formal properties of adverbs but retained the distinguishing properties of nouns. Since the reduplications stywebeen-stywebeen and witpens-witpens do not differ in regard to formal (syntactic) properties from stywebeen and witpens respectively, the reduplications would have the status of nouns too. Consequently, these reduplications would then be analyzable as noun-based noun reduplications, manifesting a lexically different type of endocentric reduplication. So, even if these reduplications could not be analyzed as adverb-based adverb reduplications, the obvious alternative would be a different endocentric analysis - not an exocentric one.

25. These endocentric analyses, of course, need not be alternatives: vang-vang and other similar forms may, on further investigation, turn out to exhibit a kind of structural ambiguity whose explanation requires both of these endocentric analyses.

26. For such analyses cf., e.g., Scholtz 1963:517, Kempen 1969:341-2, Hauptfleisch 1967:50, Raidt 1981:181.

27. As was noted above, however, lexical rules are, by their very nature, able to tolerate a certain measure of unexpected irregularity.

28. Within the framework of a traditional, nonstructuralist analysis, Bouman (1933:348) observed many years ago that forms such as brul-brul and huil-huil - taken by him to be reduplications - function like present participles when they occur in "the adverbial sentential position" [= "adverbiale zinsfunctie"].

29. Cf. Aronoff 1976:37 and Romaine 1983 for a discussion of the mode of relatedness between #ness and +ity.

30. A few present participles - e.g., verrassend (= "surprising"), spannend (= "exciting") - appear to have adverb-like correlates with lexicalized meanings.

31. Cf. Kempen 1969:289.

32. Cf. Hauptfleisch in preparation: 24.

33. Cf. Kempen 1969:289, Raidt 1981:187.

34. For expository reasons I will continue to use the term "numeral", but I do not thereby imply that it denotes a distinct lexical category that is on a par with Noun, Verb, etc.

35. In sentences with an object NP, there is in fact a second predicate position in which reduplicated "numerals" and reduplicated group/measure nouns may occur, namely after the object NP as in (ii) and (iv) below:

(i) Hy toets twee-twee studente.
he test two two students
"He tests two students at a time."
(ii) Hy toets studente twee-twee.
he test students two two
"He tests two students at a time."
(iii) Hy toets pare - pare studente.
he test pairs pairs students
"He tests the students in pairs."
(iv) Hy toets studente pare - pare.
he test students pairs pairs
"He tests the students in pairs."

As far as I can see, however, the additional position in which reduplicated "numerals" (and reduplicated group/measure nouns) may occur does not create problems of principle for the analysis proposed above.

36. As was observed in note 18 above, this conclusion cannot be attacked by citing unanalyzed "exocentric" reduplications formed irregularly by means of unproductive processes.

37. Cf., e.g., Moravscik 1978:307, 313, 324-5, Gil 1982:17-18, 208ff., Steffensen s.a.:127, Sebba 1981, Abbi to appear:3.

38. For a criticism of Lieber's view that reduplication rules, as string-dependent rules, are non-category-changing cf. Thomas-Flinders 1983:76-7. The Afrikaans formation rule (2), clearly, is not string-dependent.

39. A variant of this bracketing would be $[\alpha_i[\alpha_i]]$.

40. In Lieber's (1981:160) terminology the bracketing (120)(c) would represent the output of a "structure-building" morphological rule. She argues that the Tagalog reduplication rules need not be structure-building. For criticisms of the way in which Lieber applies the notion of "structure-building" to reduplication rules cf. Thomas-Flinders 1983:75-6.

41. One may render string (125)(c) - as well as the other ill-formed strings in (122)-(125) - acceptable by pausing between the copies and pronouncing each copy with special emphasis. The resulting utterances would, however, represent syntactic repetitions whose properties differ from those of the lexically related (morphological) reduplications.

42. On her theory of compounding Lieber (1983) would assign coffee maker the status of an "ordinary" compound. Her theory does not draw any distinction on formal grounds between so-called root/primary compounds and verbal/synthetic compounds. For informal observations on word for-

mation processes that may (not) apply iteratively cf. Bauer 1983:68.

43. As noted by Kempen (1969:489ff.) and Schultink (1974), for example, Afrikaans appears to have a rule of diminutive suffixation that may be applied to its own output, giving forms such as:

boek +	IE +	TJIE
book	DIM	DIM
boom +	PIE +	TJIE
tree	DIM	DIM

There is an analysis of forms such as these on which -*ie*/-*pie* and -*tjie* do not represent the same affix. On this analysis, whereas -*ie*/-*pie* would represent the diminutive suffix, -*tjie* would represent a distinct suffix that expresses a subjective attitude of the speaker, e.g. affection for the addressee or disparagement of the entity/entities denoted by the base. If "diminution" and "subjective attitude" were arbitrarily viewed as "two meanings of the same affix", then "the rule of diminutivization" would of course apply to its own output - though not in a sense forbidden by the Multiple Application Constraint. Also interesting in this connection are Ferguson and DeBose's (1977:106) remarks on the nonreferential or expressive function of diminution in simplified registers. Wolfgang Dressler and Peter Mühlhäusler (p.c.) have drawn my attention to forms such as the following which appear to evidence the multiple application of word formation rules:

English diminutives:	*Susiekins*, *flopsiepoos*
Polish diminutives in -*ek*:	-*ecz-ek*, -*ecz-ecz-ek*
German *vor-* and -*ur* formations:	*Ur-ur-ur ... grossmutter*, *vor-vor-vorgestern*
German compounds:	*kindeskindeskindeskinder*

Forms such as these should be analyzed in depth in a study that attempts to determine the limits of the domain within which the Multiple Application Constraint applies. For a recent systematic attempt to shed light on the nature of the phenomena on which this constraint bears cf. Rainer 1986.

44. The forms *gemaak+ongeërg* and *dik+rooi* are from Kempen 1969:186, where other, similar, compounds are presented.

45. For an analysis of this allomorphic variation cf. Botha 1968:93ff.

46. The right-hand constituent of compounds, thus, "governs" the left-hand one in the sense of Zwicky 1985. Zwicky (1985:7) characterizes "syntactic government" as "the selection of the morphosyntactic shape of one constituent (the GOVERNED, or SUBORDINATE, constituent) by virtue of its combining with another (the GOVERNOR)". He calls the "governor" "the head" of "a construct" and he extends (1985:16) these notions to morphology: "In a small class

of cases, one of the items combining in word formation bears a mark analogous to the inflectional marks of government in syntax. The other, unmarked, item is then the GOVERNOR." In this terminology, compounds in Afrikaans, unlike reduplications, exhibit a "governed constituent"-"governing constituent" structure.

47. For some discussion of the stress patterns of Afrikaans compounds cf. Botha 1968:183ff.

48. For this observation, cf., e.g., De Villiers 1969:148, Raidt 1981:78, and Scholtz 1963:149.

49. The semantics of Afrikaans reduplication will be dealt with in more detail in Chapter 3 below. For some observations on the general types of semantic relations that may hold between the main constituents of binary Afrikaans noun compounds cf. Botha 1968:164-5.

50. For the way in which the traditional semantically-based distinction between heads and modifiers has been used in syntax and morphology cf. Zwicky 1985:4, 15-16. The notion of a "semantic head" and that of a "governing head" (cf. note 48 above) should be distinguished clearly from the notion of "head" that has figured in recent theories of lexicalist morphology. As noted in §2.6 above, the latter notion is used - within the framework of a general condition such as the Endocentricity Constraint (45) - to account for the relationship of identity in lexical and "morphosyntactic" features such as gender that holds between a morphologically complex word and one of its constituents. A head in this sense constitutes, in Zwicky's (1985:18) terminology, the "morphological determinant" of a complex word.

51. For other analyses of reduplication that share Marantz's basic assumptions cf., e.g., Broselow 1983, and Broselow and McCarthy 1983/84.

52. There are weaker forms of this claim. A priori it is conceivable that the two constituents may have the same properties at some deeper level (e.g., lexical representation), yet differ in regard to certain properties at a more superficial level (e.g., phonetic representation) because of the application of certain "interpretation" rules (e.g. rules of (de-)accentuation).

53. Some morphologists - e.g. Bauer (1983:186), Botha (1980: 82-3, 140-5; 1981:18-20, 73-7), Carroll (1979:863), Dressler (1981:§4), Kageyama (1982:55), Kiparsky (1982:9-10), Savini (1983), Williams (1981:250) - have argued that WFRs must be allowed to apply to units larger than words. Others - e.g., Moody (1978) but cf. also Aronoff's (1979) reply, Kiparsky (1982:23-5) - have argued that WFRs must be allowed to apply to units smaller than words.

54. Jackendoff (1983:247, note 1) has argued that "... the open/closed class distinction is more significant to processing than to syntactic structure". If he is right, then we have identified a respect in which morphological

structure, clearly, is different from syntactic structure.

3 Semantic interpretation

1. This distinction is also found in Moravscik's (1978:317) cross-linguistic survey of the "meaning properties" of reduplications.
2. Recall that in §2.6.4 above it was argued that forms such as sing-sing in (16), staan-staan in (17), and skuifel-skuifel in (18) should be analyzed as zero derived forms rather than reduplications.
3. Cf., e.g., Bouman 1939:319, Kempen 1969:138.
4. Cf., e.g., Kempen 1969:184, 236.
5. Cf., e.g., Kempen 1969:341.
6. Cf., e.g., Kempen 1969:346.
7. Cf., e.g., Scholtz 1963:153.
8. Bouman (1939:347) assigns "attenuation" as a "meaning" to reduplications such as vaak-vaak, skaam-skaam, and traag-traag. I have been unable, however, to find any native speakers on whose interpretation a person who gets up "vaak-vaak" is less sleepy, in a referential sense, than one who gets up "vaak". The same goes for skaam-skaam and traag-traag.
9. Walter Winckler, Cecile le Roux, and Melinda Sinclair have given me considerable help in characterizing this nonreferential function of the reduplications under consideration. I will return to the meaning of these reduplications in §3.14 below. For a discussion of pragmatic - registral and/or stylistic - functions of reduplication in other languages cf., e.g., Steffensen s.a.:127-8 (Bamyili Creole) and Sebba 1981 (Sranan, etc.). Robins (1959:354), Chao (1968:204), and Cowell (1964:253) have claimed that (some) reduplications have the same referential meanings as their unreduplicated bases in the case of Sundanese, Mandarin and Syrian Arabic respectively.
10. The distinction between the real world and the projected world is drawn as follows by Jackendoff (1983:28): "If indeed the world as experienced owes so much to mental processes of organization, it is crucial for psychological theory to distinguish carefully between the source of environmental input and the world as experienced. For convenience, I will call the former the real world and the latter the projected world (experienced world or phenomenal world would also be appropriate)". [Footnote 4 omitted]
11. In his theory Jackendoff (1983:31) adopts "... a metaphysics that embraces four domains: the real world, the projected world, mental information [i.e., conceptual structure - R.P.B.], and linguistic expressions". Thus, corresponding to #water# as a real world entity, there is

an experienced entity #water# in the projected world, and corresponding to this latter entity there is a conceptual constituent [WATER] which, in turn, is expressed by the linguistic form "water".

12. For the relation between the concept of countability and that of boundedness cf., e.g., Jackendoff 1983:246, n. 9.

13. To illustrate the distinction, Jackendoff (1983:246, n. 9) contrasts the following utterances:

(i) Oil was leaking onto / all over the floor.

(ii) Some oil was leaking onto / ??all over the floor.

He observes that "(i) presents the oil as a more or less continuous stream, or unbounded quantity within the time-frame described by the utterance. By contrast, (ii) presents the oil as a bounded quantity. This difference is related to the oddness of 'all over' in (ii)."

14. In addition to a group or collective sense, *tien* and *drie* have an individual or noncollective sense as well: [NINE PLUS ONE INDIVIDUALLY] in the case of *tien*, and [TWO PLUS ONE INDIVIDUALLY] in the case of *drie*. For some observations on the so-called "individual-collective distinction" cf. Gil 1982:55-6.

15. On Lyons's (1977:483) analysis an act is an event that is under control of an agent.

16. As has been noted by, for example, Holisky (1981:28) "The term 'aspect' has almost as many definitions as there are linguists who have used it ...". Platzack (1979:39) draws a distinction between aspect and *aktionsart*:

"Whereas aktionsart has to do with the inherent temporal constitution of a situation, independent of deictic time (i.e., time in its relation to speaker and hearer), we will use the term *aspect* to refer to the way a speaker (or writer) chooses to present a situation in relation to deictic time, provided that the language offers a systematic way to express the choice in question. Thus, aspect is intimately connected to the use of a sentence (or, as we will prefer to say, to the possible use of a sentence). To describe the aktionsart referred to by a sentence, we do not have to take into consideration how the sentence is related to the communicative situation (though such a relation may be taken into consideration when we like to disambiguate a sentence in cases where a given string of words is able to refer to several aktionsarten). However, in order to describe the aspect of a sentence, this relation is of utmost importance."

I will use the term *aspect*, and a derived form such as *aspectual*, to denote Platzack's *aktionsart*. This is a common usage of the term *aspect*, as is clear from Comrie's (1976:3) discussion in which he presents "a general definition of aspect" according to which "aspects are different ways of viewing the internal temporal constituency of a situation", a definition attributed by him to Holt (1943:6). For remarks on the history of the aspectual notion of "boundedness" cf., e.g., Platzack 1979: 70ff., and Dahl 1981:79-81. For critical comments on Platzack's distinction between aspect and aktionsart cf. Andersson 1984:200ff.

17. As has been noted by a number of linguists, most recently by Jackendoff (1983), there is a parallelism between iterating events and increasing things in number. At a linguistic level, therefore, "iterativity" and "plurality" are fundamentally similar notions. Platzack (1979:79ff.) and others use the semantic feature "+/-DIVID" as a semantic correlate of Chomsky's (1965) syntactic feature "+/-COUNT". Following Teleman (1969), Platzack (1979:81) argues that the feature "DIVID" is useful for capturing the "count-mass" distinction in the description of (Swedish) noun phrases. Teleman suggests that this feature can be used for the description of verbs too, with "-DIVID" assigned to "durative" verbs. However, Platzack argues that the feature should not be assigned to the verb, but to the sentence, because it is the situation corresponding to the sentence that should be described in terms of aktionsarten. For a further illustration of the explanatory power of the notion of "boundedness" cf. Heinämäki 1984:155ff.

18. In a study of Swedish aktionsarten, Platzack (1979: 124ff.) too argues that "iterativity" and "durativity" are not fundamental notions. Bridgen (1984) similarly argues that in Finnish iterativity and habituality are not basic aspectual notions.

19. For some discussion of Vendler's notion of "achievement" - and his related but distinct notion of "accomplishment" - cf. Lyons 1977:711-12, Holisky 1981:133ff., and Mourelatos 1981:191ff. Accomplishments (such as to run a mile, to paint a picture, to grow up, etc.) and achievements differ in that the former, but not the latter, have intrinsic duration. Recently, Jackendoff (to appear:7) has postulated the binary semantic feature [± Closed] to differentiate between Ordinary location (as expressed by Some water was on the floor) and Distributive location (as expressed by Water was all over the floor). He (p. 12), moreover, speculates that this feature "appears also in the semantic structure of Events, indicating this time temporal closure or lack thereof. Achievements and accomplishments (in the sense of Vendler (1967)), which have a temporal endpoint, would be [+ Closed]; processes which are conceptualized without temporal endpoints, would be [- Closed]."

20. For some observations on the notion of "quality" cf. Lyons 1977:711-12.

21. Specifying the functions under consideration appears to be part of a description of what Chomsky (1980:59) calls "pragmatic competence". Katz (1972:434-5) also would apparently not specify such functions in the kind of se-

mantic component he envisages. He provides for the possibility of developing a "rhetorical component" within which "matters of rhetoric and style may be accounted for".

22. Jackendoff (1983:19) contends, by implication, that there cannot be a level of autonomous semantics of the type provided for by Katz, since there are no primitives and/or principles of combination appropriate to the formalization of linguistic inference that are distinct from those appropriate to the communication of visual information to the linguistic system.

23. For earlier examples of such rules, cf. Jackendoff 1972.

24. In their analysis of "the logic of the English progressive", Goldsmith and Woisetschlaeger (1982) draw a distinction between the "aspectual" or "imperfective use" and the "metaphysical use" of the progressive. As regards the mutual interrelatedness of these two "uses" of the progressive, they (1982:80, n. 2) observe that

"The metaphysical use of the progressive ... is the automatic result, we believe, of the extension of the use of the imperfective marker to an 'axis of being', in Whorf's (1956) terminology. Propositions, the objects of our knowledge, are viewed as relatively closer to or farther from the 'essence' or 'heart' (again, in Whorf's terminology) of the aspect of the universe which they describe. The ultimate object of human knowledge being understanding, rather than mere description, a proposition which has reached the endpoint on the metaphysical axis - which is therefore expressed through a perfective aspect - will be one which specifies the structure of the universe, not merely its observed constituents."

And: "It is our view that the kind of unabashed mixture of philosophical reflection, ethnographic description, and linguistic analysis which we have found in Whorf (1956) is necessary to do serious linguistic semantics." The construal presented by Goldsmith and Woisetschlaeger of the relationship holding between the "aspectual" and the "metaphysical use" of the English progressive appears to me of the sort that can be naturally expressed by means of conceptualization rules. Though they do not explicitly invoke conceptualization rules in their analysis of "the logic of the English progressive", Goldsmith and Woisetschlaeger more than once allude to the way in which speakers "conceptualize situations" or "states of affairs".

For example: "The endpoint for other episodes is not as clear, and is more evidently imposed by the way the speaker conceptualizes the situation. For example, John ran along the beach this morning may well be spoken (and true) whether or not John's run had an endpoint defined in advance. This becomes clearer when one notices that whenever we say John was running along the beach, we are implicitly assuming that at the point we speak of, John had not reached the natural endpoint of his run" (p. 79).

It appears to me that what we have in such observations are implicit appeals by Goldsmith and Woisetschlaeger to conceptualization rules of the type discussed above.

25. Thus, Ray Jackendoff (p.c.) has observed that these rules "... look ad hoc, though of course they are not - they're the most natural thing in the world ...".

26. How such contextual disambiguation actually proceeds is a complex question that lies beyond the scope of the present study. For suggestive observations cf., e.g., Kess and Hopper's (1985) discussion of the role of shared knowledge and of Rosch's (1973, 1975, 1977) lexical hierarchies in disambiguation.

27. Gil's (1982:228) general conclusion reads as follows: "Semantically, we found that the effect of reduplication is, almost always, to force the reduplicated expression to distribute over another constituent - most often phrase internally, but sometimes also clausally" [Footnote 16 omitted].

28. It is not claimed that every lexical item that may be reduplicated should be independently quantifiable too. It would be strange indeed if the behavior of some lexical items did not exhibit a measure of idiosyncrasy.

29. For some discussion of this thesis cf. Botha 1984a:131.

30. There is a secondary aspect to this iconicity: in the case of certain (but not all) reduplications a scattering of the (increased) form corresponds to a scattering of the (increased) referents. Notice, incidentally, that partial reduplication is less likely to be motivated. Mayerthaler (1977:28, 33ff.), however, has argued that iconicity is a property of partial reduplications that express diminution.

31. It should be kept in mind, though, that Afrikaans has processes of syntactic repetition which copy larger syntactic constituents such as noun phrases. An analysis of the semantics of these processes could reveal that, in order to distinguish between the semantic rules and principles applying to copied syntactic constituents and those formulated above for reduplications, the latter rules and principles have to be formulated so as to refer to the (lexical) category status of the constituents of reduplications. Such a finding would furnish some support for the Category Retention Constraint. It is also possible, of course that the rules that assign stress to Afrikaans reduplications may require that the constituents of these complex forms be assigned a particular (lexical) category status.

32. For a recent analysis that attempts to depict "the correlations between verb aspect and nominal reference" as "straightforward consequences of what is known of the aspect of atomic sentences on the one hand and the logic of natural language quantification on the other hand" cf. Carlson 1981. Other analyses that attempt to account for what Carlson (1981:48) calls "important analogies between

reference in the object domain and in the temporal domain" are those by Vendler (1967), Taylor (1977), and Mourelatos (1981:202ff.). An earlier attempt to show in some detail and with reference to a considerable number of languages that "nominale Pluralität" and "verbale Pluralität" are "homomorph" is found in Dressler 1968.

33. One of the few analyses of the semantics of reduplication that have been carried out within a more or less coherent theoretical framework is the one by Idris (1981) of the "semantic properties" of verbal reduplication in Amharic, Hindi, Malay, Salish dialects and Siroi. The framework chosen for this analysis is the one developed by Chafe in his <u>Meaning and the structure of language</u> (1970).

4 Link-up

1. The essence of the matter may be stated in an alternative, empirically nondistinct way: the proposed set of conceptualization rules does not include rules that provide conceptual structures corresponding to all the reduplications jointly generated by the formation rule and the interpretation rule. In terms of this formulation, a reduplication is "filtered out" as conceptually impossible by its not being assigned a conceptual structure by the proposed conceptualization rules.

References

Abbi, A. to appear. Reduplicative structures: a phenomenon of the South Asian linguistic area. Mimeographed.

Adams, V. 1973. An introduction to modern English word-formation. London: Longman.

Aitchison, J. 1985. Cognitive clouds and semantic shadows. Language and Communication 5:69-93.

Allen, M.R. 1978. Morphological investigations. Ph.D. Dissertation, University of Connecticut.

Anderson, S. 1982. Where is morphology? Linguistic Inquiry 13: 571-612.

Andersson, S-G. 1984. What is aspectual about the perfect and the pluperfect in Swedish? In De Groot and Tommola (eds.) 1984:199-207.

Aronoff, M. 1976. Word-formation in generative grammar. Linguistic Inquiry Monograph One. Cambridge, Mass.: MIT Press.

Aronoff, M. 1979. A reply to Moody. Glossa 13:115-18.

Aronoff, M. 1980. Contextuals. Language 56:744-58.

Aronoff, M. 1982. Potential words, actual words, productivity and frequency. Preprints of Plenary Session, Thirteenth International Congress of Linguists, Tokyo, pp. 141-8.

Bauer, L. 1983. English word-formation. Cambridge: Cambridge University Press.

Binnick, R.I., Davidson, A., Green, G., Morgan, J. (eds.). 1969. Papers from the Fifth Regional Meeting of the Chicago Linguistic Society. Chicago.

Botha, R.P. 1964. Voorstudie tot 'n klassifikasie van Afrikaanse komposita. M.A.-Tesis, Universiteit van Stellenbosch, Stellenbosch.

Botha, R.P. 1968. The function of the lexicon in transformational generative grammar. Janua Linguarum, Series Maior 38. The Hague and Paris: Mouton.

Botha, R.P. 1973. The justification of linguistic hypotheses. A study of nondemonstrative inference in transformational grammar. Janua Linguarum, Series Maior 84. The Hague and Paris: Mouton.

Botha, R.P. 1980. Word-based morphology and synthetic compounding. Stellenbosch Papers in Linguistics 5. Stellenbosch, Department of General Linguistics, U.S.

Botha, R.P. 1981. A base rule theory of Afrikaans synthetic compounding. In Moortgat et al. (eds.) 1981:1-77.

Botha, R.P. 1982. On 'the Galilean style' of linguistic inquiry. Lingua 58:1-50.

Botha, R.P. 1984a. Morphological mechanisms. Lexicalist analyses of synthetic compounding. Language and Communication Library, Volume 7. Oxford, etc.: Pergamon Press.

Botha, R.P. 1984b. A Galilean analysis of Afrikaans reduplication. Stellenbosch Papers in Linguistics 13. Stellenbosch, Department of General Linguistics, U.S.

Botha, R.P., and Sinclair, M. to appear. Brame on Chomsky's epistemological tolerance. Stellenbosch Papers in Linguistics.

Bouman, A.C. 1939. Over reduplicatie en de woordsoorten. De Nieuwe Taalgids 33:337-53.

Brame, M. 1985. Universal induction and Move α. Linguistic Analysis 14:313-52.

Bresnan, J. 1982. The mental representation of grammatical relations. Cambridge, Mass.: MIT Press.

Bridgen, N. 1984. Towards a functional grammar of aspect in Finnish. In De Groot and Tommola (eds.) 1984: 179-98.

Broselow, E. 1983. Salish double reduplications: subjacency in morphology. Natural Language and Linguistic Theory 1:317-46.

Broselow, E., and McCarthy, J. 1983/84. A theory of internal reduplication. The Linguistic Review 3:25-88.

Carlson, L. 1981. Aspect and quantification. In Tedeschi and Zaenen (eds.) 1981:31-64.

Carrier, J. 1979. The interaction of phonological and morphological rules in Tagalog: A study in the relationship between rule components in grammar. Ph.D. Dissertation, MIT, Cambridge, Mass.

Carroll, J.M. 1979. Complex compounds: phrasal embedding in lexical structures. Linguistics 17:863-77.

Chafe, W.L. 1970. Meaning and the structure of language. Chicago: University of Chicago Press.

Chao, Y.R. 1968. A grammar of spoken Chinese. Berkeley, etc.: University of California Press.

Chomsky, N. 1965. Aspects of the theory of syntax. Cambridge, Mass.: MIT Press.

Chomsky, N. 1970. Remarks on nominalization. In Jacobs and Rosenbaum (eds.) 1970:184-221.

Chomsky, N. 1980. Rules and representations. New York: Columbia University Press.

Chomsky, N. 1981. Lectures on government and binding. Dordrecht: Foris Publications.

Clark, E.V., and Clark, H.H. 1979. When nouns surface as verbs. Language 55:767-811.

Coetzee, A.J. (ed.). 1981. Hulsels van kristal: Bundel aangebied aan Ernst van Heerden by geleentheid van sy vyfen-sestigste verjaardag op 20 Maart 1981. Kaapstad: Tafelberg.

Cole, P., and Morgan, J.L. (eds.). 1975. Syntax and semantics III: Speech acts. New York: Academic Press.

Comrie, B. 1976. Aspect. An introduction to the study of verbal aspect and related problems. Cambridge, etc.: Cambridge University Press.

Cowell, M.W. 1964. A reference grammar of Syrian Arabic. Washington, D.C.: Georgetown University Press.

Culicover, P.T., Wasow, T., and Akmajian, A. (eds.). 1977. Formal syntax. New York, etc.: Academic Press.

Dahl, Ö. 1981. On the definition of the telic-atelic (bounded-nonbounded) distinction. In Tedeschi and Zaenen (eds.) 1981:79-90.

De Groot, C., and Tommola, H. (eds.). 1984. Aspect bound. A voyage into the realm of Germanic, Slavonic and Finno-Ugrian aspectology. Dordrecht: Foris Publications.

De Villiers, M. 1969. Afrikaanse klankleer: fonetiek, fonologie en woordbou. Vyfde Druk. Kaapstad: Balkema.

Dressler, W.U. 1968. Studien zur verbalen Pluralität. Iterativum, Distributivum, Durativum, Intensivum in der allgemeinen Grammatik, im Lateinischen und Hethitischen. Österreichische Akademie der Wissenschaften, Philosophisch-Historische Klasse, Sitzungsberichte, 259, Band 1. Abhandlung. Wien: Hermann Böhlaus Nachf.

Dressler, W.U. 1981. On word formation in natural morphology. Wiener Linguistische Gazette 26:3-14.

Ferguson, C.A., and DeBose, C.E. 1977. Simplified registers, broken language, and pidginization. In Valdman (ed.) 1977:99-125.

Gil, D. 1982. Distributive numerals. Ph.D. Dissertation, University of California, Los Angeles. Published on demand by University Microfilms International, Ann Arbor & London.

Gleason Jr., H.A. 1965. Linguistics and English grammar. New York: Holt, Rinehart & Winston.

Goldsmith, J., and Woisetschlaeger, E. 1982. The logic of the English progressive. Linguistic Inquiry 13:79-98.

Greenberg, J.H. (ed.) 1978. Universals of human language. Volume 3. Stanford: Stanford University Press.

Grice, H.P. 1975. Logic and conversation. In Cole and Morgan (eds.) 1975:41-58.

Halle, M. 1973. Prolegomena to a theory of word formation. Linguistic Inquiry 4:3-16.

Hauptfleisch, D.C. 1967. Twee 'Afrikaanse' iteratiewe in Nederlands. Standpunte 20:50-7.

Hauptfleisch, D.C. in preparation. Woordherhaling en reduplikasie in Afrikaans. Doktorale proefskrif, Universiteit van Stellenbosch, Stellenbosch.

Heinämäki, O. 1984. Aspect in Finnish. In De Groot and Tommola (eds.) 1984:153-77.

Holisky, D.A. 1981. Aspect theory and Georgian aspect. In Tedeschi and Zaenen (eds.) 1981:127-44.

Holt, J. 1943. *Etudes d'aspect*. *Acta Jutlandica* 15/2.

Idris, A.A. 1981. The semantic structure of verbal reduplication: a case study of reduplication in Amharic, Hindi, Malay, Salish and Siroi. *Kansas Working Papers in Linguistics* 6:17-41.

Jackendoff, R.S. 1972. *Semantic interpretation in generative grammar*. Cambridge, Mass.: MIT Press.

Jackendoff, R.S. 1975. Morphological and semantic regularities in the lexicon. *Language* 51:639-71.

Jackendoff, R.S. 1977. *X syntax: a study of phrase structure*. *Linguistic Inquiry Monograph Two*. Cambridge, Mass.: MIT Press.

Jackendoff, R.S. 1981. On Katz's autonomous semantics. *Language* 57:425-35.

Jackendoff, R.S. 1983. *Semantics and cognition*. *Current Studies in Linguistics Series* 8. Cambridge, Mass.: MIT Press.

Jackendoff, R.S. to appear. Distributive location. *Sophia Linguistica*.

Jacobs, R.A., and Rosenbaum, P.S. (eds.). 1970. *Readings in English transformational grammar*. Waltham, Mass.: Ginn and Co.

Jazayery, M.A., Polomé, E.C., and Winter, W. (eds.). 1978. *Linguistic and literary studies in honor of Archibald A. Hill*. *II Descriptive Linguistics*. The Hague, Paris and New York: Mouton Publishers.

Kageyama, J. 1982. Word formation in Japanese. *Lingua* 57:215-58.

Katz, J.J. 1972. *Semantic theory*. New York: Harper and Row.

Katz, J.J. 1980. Chomsky on meaning. *Language* 56:1-41.

Katz, J.J. 1981. *Language and other abstract objects*. Oxford: Basil Blackwell.

Kempen, W. 1969. *Samestelling, afleiding, en woordsoortelike meerfunksionaliteit in Afrikaans*. Tweede en hersiene druk van *Woordvorming en funksiewisseling in Afrikaans*. Kaapstad, ens.: Nasou Beperk.

Kess, J.F., and Hopper, R.A. 1985. Bias, individual differences, and 'shared knowledge' in ambiguity. Journal of Pragmatics 9: 21-39.

Kiparsky, P. 1982. Lexical morphology and phonology. In Linguistics in the Morning Calm: 3-91. Seoul: Hanskin Publishing Company.

Kiparsky, P. 1983. Word-formation and the lexicon. Mimeographed. [To appear in F. Ingeman (ed.). Proceedings of the 1982 Mid-America Linguistics Conference, University of Kansas, Lawrence, K.S.]

Lieber, R. 1981. On the organization of the lexicon. Reproduced by the Indiana University Linguistics Club, Bloomington.

Lieber, R. 1983. Argument-linking and compounds in English. Linguistic Inquiry 14: 251-285.

Lyons, J. 1977. Semantics. Volume 1 and 2. Cambridge, etc.: Cambridge University Press.

Marantz, A. 1981. On the nature of grammatical relations. Ph.D. Dissertation, MIT, Cambridge, Mass.

Marantz, A. 1982. Re reduplication. Linguistic Inquiry 13:435-482.

Marchand, H. 1969. The categories and types of present-day English word-formation. Second edition. München: Beck.

Mayerthaler, W. 1977. Studien zur theoretischen und zur französischen Morphologie. Tübingen: Max Niemeyer Verlag.

McCarthy, J.J. 1979. Formal problems in Semitic phonology and morphology. Ph.D. Dissertation, MIT, Cambridge, Mass.

McCarthy, J.J. 1981. A prosodic theory of nonconcatenative morphology. Linguistic Inquiry 12:373-418.

Miller, G.A., and Johnson-Laird, P.N. 1976. Language and perception. Cambridge, Mass.: The Belknap Press of Harvard University Press.

Moody, M.D. 1978. Some preliminaries to a theory of morphology. Glossa 12:16-38.

Moore, T.E. (ed.). 1973. Cognitive development and the acquisition of language. New York, San Francisco, London: Academic Press.

Moortgat, H.M., van der Hulst, H., and Hoekstra, T. (eds.). 1981. The scope of lexical rules. Linguistic Models 1. Dordrecht: Foris Publications.

Moravscik, E.A. 1978. Reduplicative constructions. In Greenberg (ed.) 1978:297-334.

Mourelatos, A.P.D. 1981. Events, processes, and states. In Tedeschi and Zaenen (eds.) 1981:191-212.

Pike, K.L. 1967. Language in relation to a unified theory of the structure of human behavior. Second, revised edition. Janua Linguarum, Series Maior 24. The Hague: Mouton.

Platzack, C. 1979. The semantic interpretation of aspect and aktionsarten. A study of internal time reference in Swedish. Dordrecht: Foris Publications.

Postal, P.M. 1969. Anaphoric islands. In Binnick et al. (eds.) 1969:205-239.

Quirk, R., Greenbaum, S., Leech, G., and Svartvik, J. 1972. A grammar of contemporary English. London: Longman.

Radford, A. 1981. Transformational syntax. A student's guide to Chomsky's Extended Standard Theory. Cambridge: Cambridge University Press.

Raidt, E.H. 1980. Die Reduplikation im Afrikaans. In Rupp and Roloff (eds.) 1980:494-501.

Raidt, E.H. 1981. Oor die herkoms van die Afrikaanse reduplikasie. In Coetzee (ed.) 1981:178-89.

Rainer, F. 1986. Recursiveness in word-formation. Paper read at the International Conference on Theoretical Approaches to Morphology held at Veszprém (Hungary), 1-4 May 1986.

Robins, A.H. 1959. Nominal and verbal derivation in Sundanese. Lingua 8:337-69.

Roeper, T., and Siegel, M. 1978. A lexical transformation for verbal compounds. Linguistic Inquiry 9:199-260.

Romaine, S. 1983. On the productivity of word formation rules and limits of variability in the lexicon. Australian Journal of Linguistics 3:177-200.

Rosch, E.H. 1973. On the internal structure of perceptual and semantic categories. In Moore (ed.) 1973:111-114.

Rosch, E.H. 1975. Cognitive representations of semantic categories. Journal of Experimental Psychology 104:192-233.

Rosch, E.H. 1977. Human categorization. In Warren (ed.) 1977: 3-49.

Rupp, H., and Roloff, H-G. (eds.). 1980. Akten des VI. Internationalen Germanisten-Kongresses Basel 1980. Bern, etc.: Peter Lang.

Samarin, W.J. 1978. Inventory and choice in expressive language. In Jazayery, Polomé, Winter (eds.) 1978:313-29.

Savini, M. 1983. Phrasal compounds in Afrikaans: a generative analysis. M.A. Thesis, University of Stellenbosch, Stellenbosch.

Scholtz, J. du P. 1963. Reduplikasieverskynsels in Afrikaans. In his Taalhistoriese Opstelle. Pretoria: J.L. van Schaik.

Schultink, H. 1974. Dubbele diminutieven in het Afrikaans en transformationeel-generatieve taalbeschrijving. In Taalkunde - 'n lewe. Studies opgedra aan prof. dr. W. Kempen by geleentheid van sy 65ste verjaardag. Kaapstad, ens.: Tafelberg-Uitgewers.

Sebba, M. 1981. Derivational regularities in a Creole lexicon: the case of Sranan. Linguistics 19:101-117.

Selkirk, E.O. 1982. The syntax of words. Linguistic Inquiry Monograph Seven. Cambridge, Mass.: MIT Press.

Siegel, D. 1974. Topics in English morphology. Ph.D. Dissertation, MIT, Cambridge, Mass.

Simpson, J. 1983. Interaction of morphology and syntax. Paper presented at GLOW conference, York, England, March 1983.

Sinclair, M. 1985. The rationality of Chomsky's linguistics (= Stellenbosch Papers in Linguistics 14). Stellenbosch: Department of General Linguistics.

Steffensen, M.S. s.a. Reduplication in Bamyili Creole. In Papers in Pidgin and Creole Linguistics No. 2. Department of Linguistics, Research School of Pacific Studies, The Australian National University.

Taylor, B. 1977. Tense and continuity. Linguistics and Philosophy 1:199-220.

Tedeschi, P.J., and Zaenen, A. (eds.). 1981. Tense and aspect. Syntax and Semantics, Volume 14. New York, etc.: Academic Press.

Teleman, U. 1969. Definita och indefinita attribut u nusvenskan: Lund: Studentlitteratur.

Theron, A.S. 1974. Aspekte van meerfunksionaliteit in Afrikaans. Doktorale Proefskrif, Universiteit van Stellenbosch, Stellenbosch.

Thomas-Flinders, T.G. 1983. Morphological structures. Ph.D. Dissertation, University of California, Los Angeles.

Todd, L. 1974. Pidgins and creoles. London and Boston: Routledge & Kegan Paul.

Valdman, A. (ed.). 1977. Pidgin and creole linguistics. Bloomington & London: Indiana University Press.

Vendler, Z. 1967. Linguistics in philosophy. Ithaca, New York: Cornell University Press.

Warren, N. (ed.). 1977. Studies in cross-cultural psychology. London, New York, San Francisco: Academic Press.

Wasow, T. 1977. Transformations and the lexicon. In Culicover et al. (eds.) 1977:327-60.

Williams, E. 1981. On the notions 'lexically related' and 'head of a word'. Linguistic Inquiry 12:245-74.

Zwicky, A.M. 1985. Heads. Journal of Linguistics 21:1-29.

Index

For EU product safety concerns, contact us at Calle de José Abascal, 56–1°, 28003 Madrid, Spain or eugpsr@cambridge.org.

www.ingramcontent.com/pod-product-compliance
Ingram Content Group UK Ltd.
Pitfield, Milton Keynes, MK11 3LW, UK
UKHW010046140625
459647UK00012BB/1648

* 9 7 8 0 5 2 1 0 2 6 1 3 0 *